HAMPTON-BROWN
HIGH POINT

SUCCESS IN LANGUAGE • LITERATURE • CONTENT

Grammar Practice Book

LEVEL B

HAMPTON-BROWN

Complete Sentences

A **complete sentence** has a subject and a predicate.

- The **complete subject** includes all the words that tell about the subject.

Examples: My art teacher | draws pictures.
complete subject

Mrs. Jones | likes to draw.
complete subject

- The **complete predicate** includes all the words in the predicate part of the sentence.

Examples: She | draws shapes.
complete predicate

She | colors the pictures.
complete predicate

The students | like her pictures.
complete subject ➕ **complete predicate**

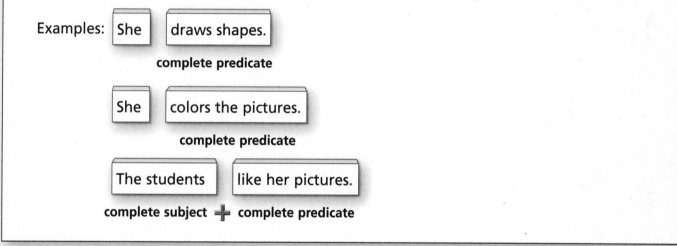

A. Circle the complete subject in each sentence. Underline the complete predicate.

1. (My art class) is a lot of fun.

2. (The students) work hard.

3. (Our teacher) helps us.

4. (My friend Juan) paints animals.

5. (His animals) look so real!

6. (Juan) painted a funny picture.

7. (One lion) had a big smile.

8. (I) like his pictures very much!

9. (They) are very colorful.

Complete Sentences, continued

B. Complete each sentence with a subject or a predicate from one of the boxes, or add your own. Write it on the line.

10. My best painting _____ looks like a park _____

   _____ .

11. _____

   Wild flower _____ grow in the garden.

12. Little white ducks _are swimming in the lake_

   _____ .

13. _____

   _____ The kid _____ play ball.

14. The sun _was really hot_ _____

   _____ .

15. Everyone _was having fun_ _____

   _____ .

Complete Subjects
Beautiful flowers
Some children
Green bushes
Two families
My best painting

Complete Predicates
looks like a park
swim in the lake
shines brightly
looks happy
run around

C. Add a complete subject or complete predicate to make a complete sentence.

16. _____ My favorite artist _____ uses bright colors.

17. The people in her paintings _are always laughing_ .

18. My mother _like her painting to_ .

19. A shop near us _sale bright color paint._ .

20. _My mom and i_ _____ went to the shop.

21. We _brought a lot of artistic stuff_ .

22. _My favorite artist was at the shop_ _____ was at the shop.

23. I _was amazed._ !

D. 24.–26. Tell a partner about an artist that you have heard of. Is the artist creative? Use three complete sentences.

Example: "The artist paints wild animals."

4

Common and Proper Nouns

A noun names a person, place, thing, or idea. There are many kinds of nouns.

- A **common noun** names any person, place, thing, or idea. A **proper noun** names one particular person, place, thing, or idea.

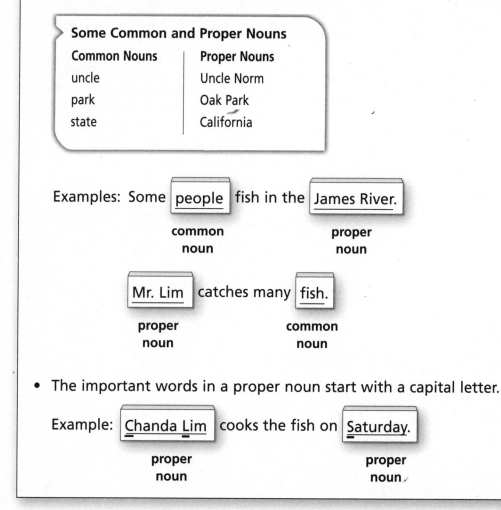

> **Some Common and Proper Nouns**
>
> | Common Nouns | Proper Nouns |
> |---|---|
> | uncle | Uncle Norm |
> | park | Oak Park |
> | state | California |

Examples: Some | people | fish in the | James River. |

                 common   proper

                  noun   noun

| Mr. Lim | catches many | fish. |

  proper   common

    noun   noun

- The important words in a proper noun start with a capital letter.

Example: | Chanda Lim | cooks the fish on | Saturday. |

    proper   proper

     noun   noun

A. Read each sentence. Circle each proper noun. Underline each common noun.

1. One (Sunday) my <u>family</u> took a <u>trip</u>.

2. My friend Jose came, too.

3. We drove to the city of Austin.

4. I saw the Colorado River.

5. Jose said, "Mr. Lopez, can we go in the water?"

6. My dad said, "Yes. We will take a boat on Lake Austin. The river flows into it."

7. Jose said, "I will tell our teacher, Mrs. Chou, about this fun day."

Common and Proper Nouns, continued

B. Read the passage. Underline all the nouns. Then write the nouns in the chart where they belong. Write each noun only one time.

"Hello and welcome to California! My name is Ester. This is our bus. I am your guide. I am the driver, too! I hope you like our state. You can see many beautiful flowers and trees in our parks.

This is San Francisco. Many people live here. It is a big city! You can see visitors and workers. People come here from China, Mexico, and many other countries. Golden Gate Park is beautiful. You can see San Francisco Bay, too. There are big farms near the city. Grapes and cotton grow on the farms."

Common Nouns		Proper Nouns
8. name	16.	24. California
9.	17.	25.
10.	18.	26.
11.	19.	27.
12.	20.	28.
13.	21.	29.
14.	22.	30.
15.	23.	

C. Complete the paragraphs. Add common nouns in the first paragraph. Add proper nouns in the second paragraph.

Mr. Ortiz works on a _____farm_____ . He picks _____ . His
                          31.   **32.**

_____ , Mr. Chan, works there, too. They work hard in the _____
    33.   **34.**

all day. Sometimes Mr. Ortiz gets _____ from his son, Carlos.
                                        35.

On _____ the men had a day off. They went to the town of _____ .
       36.   **37.**

They caught fish in the _____ . They ate hamburgers at _____ . "I like
                              38.   **39.**

the weather in _____ . It is nice and warm," said Mr. Ortiz.
                    40.

Singular and Plural Nouns

A **noun** names a person, a place, a thing, or an idea. There are many kinds of nouns.

- A **singular noun** names one person, place, thing, or idea. A **plural noun** names more than one.

> **Some Singular and Plural Nouns**
>
> | Singular Nouns | Plural Nouns |
> |---|---|
> | poem | poems |
> | interview | interviews |
> | artist | artists |

Example: My favorite | poet | writes many funny | poems.

         singular   **plural**
          noun   **noun**

- A **count noun** is a noun that you can count. A **noncount noun** is a noun that you cannot count.

Example: He wrote about a | bowl | of | cereal.

         count   **noncount**
        noun   **noun**

- A count noun has a plural form. A noncount noun does not have a plural form.

Example: The | apples | gave him | energy.

     plural count   **noncount**
        noun   **noun**

A. Write "count" or "noncount" to tell about the underlined noun.

1. <u>Cereal</u> is good to eat.   <u>noncount</u>

2. It usually comes in a <u>box</u>.   _____

3. You can put it in a <u>bowl</u> to eat it.   _____

4. You eat it with a <u>spoon</u>.   _____

5. It gives you a lot of <u>energy</u>.   _____

Singular and Plural Nouns, continued

B. Read the passage. Underline all the common nouns. Then write the nouns in the chart where they belong. Write each noun only one time.

José sent a note to me. "Marta, I feel much love for you," it said. It made my heart happy. Now I will make cookies for him! He likes cereal. So I will make cookies from cereal and apples. I will make them in funny shapes. There will be a mermaid and a kangaroo. Some cookies will look like giraffes and bunnies. We will eat them after lunch. We will have lemonade, too. The cookies will be good fuel. They will give him energy. José will say, "Marta, I like your creativity!"

Singular Count Nouns	Plural Count Nouns	Noncount Nouns
6. note	11.	16.
7.	12.	17.
8.	13.	18.
9.	14.	19.
10.	15.	20.
		21.

C. 22.–27. Edit the journal entry below. Make sure the count and noncount nouns are used correctly.

Journal Entry

July 19

Yesterday we went to the river. First Olivia and I went into the water. We swam like mermaid. We got all wet! Then we put on dry clothings. After that we had our lunch on the shore. We each ate two hamburgers and ten grape. Suddenly we heard loud thunders. We ran to the car. Then the rain started. "That was good lucks," I said. We had fun and stayed dry. We will go to the rivers again soon. Maybe we will have a picnic, too!

Revising and Editing Marks

∧	Add.
↻	Move to here.
⌐	Replace with this.
⌿	Take out.
⌃	Add a comma.
⊙	Add a period.
≡	Capitalize.
/	Make lower case.

© Hampton-Brown

Singular and Plural Nouns

Count nouns are nouns that you can count. The **singular** form means "one." The **plural** form means "more than one."

How to Form the Plural of Count Nouns

- Add **–s** to most count nouns. If the noun ends in **x, ch, sh, s,** or **z,** add **–es.**
- For nouns that end in a consonant plus **y,** change the **y** to **i** and add **–es.**
- For nouns that end in a vowel plus **y,** just add **–s.**
- For most nouns that end in **f** or **fe,** change the **f** to **v** and add **–es.** For some nouns that end in **f,** just add **–s.**
- If the noun ends in a vowel plus **o,** add **–s.** Nouns that end in a consonant plus **o,** add **–s.** For others, add **–es.**

Examples:

The poet read his poems to us	while we ate our lunches.
add –s	add –es

They were wonderful stories.	We would have listened for days.
change y to i and add –es	add –s

His poems changed our lives.	He is one of our heroes.
change f to v and add –es	consonant plus o add –es

- A few count nouns have irregular plural forms.

Example:

The children enjoyed	his poem about the trout.
irregular plural form	same singular and plural form

A. Read each singular noun. Draw a line to the plural form.

Singular Nouns	Plural Nouns
1. bunch	men
2. river	rivers
3. essay	months
4. man	bunches
5. month	essays

Singular and Plural Nouns, continued

B. Write the correct form of the plural for each singular noun in parentheses.

6. The government wanted to remember the _____soldiers_____ of the Vietnam War. (**soldier**)

7. A special park in Washington, D. C., already had many _____ in it. (**memorial**)

8. The government had a contest to design the memorial. They got many _____ . (**design**)

9. Maya Lin and other _____ entered the contest. (**artist**)

10. There were many great _____ . (**idea**)

11. The _____ liked her design the best. (**judge**)

12. The Vietnam Veterans Memorial is over 246 _____ long. (**foot**)

13. Many _____ visit the memorial each year. (**student**)

14. They read the many _____ on the wall. (**name**)

C. 15.–20. Edit the journal entry below. Make sure each noun is in the correct singular or plural form and is spelled correctly.

Journal Entry

June 1

In May I went to Washington, D. C., for four day. I saw many interesting places. I have so many memorys of my visit to the Vietnam Veterans Memorial. The wall is so long! I read the names of some of the soldieres. It would take many hour to read them all. I thought about these man and women. They are all hero to me.

Revising and Editing Marks	
∧	Add.
⤳	Move to here.
⤻	Replace with this.
໑	Take out.
⌃	Add a comma.
⊙	Add a period.
=	Capitalize.
/	Make lower case.

© Hampton-Brown

Possessive Nouns

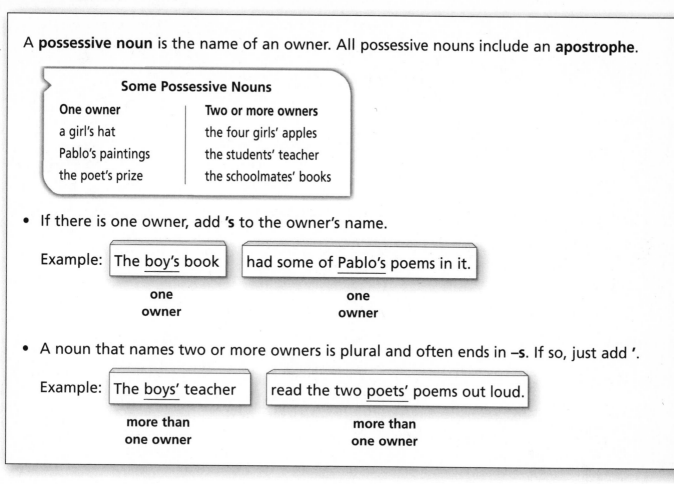

A **possessive noun** is the name of an owner. All possessive nouns include an **apostrophe**.

Some Possessive Nouns

One owner	Two or more owners
a girl's hat	the four girls' apples
Pablo's paintings	the students' teacher
the poet's prize	the schoolmates' books

- If there is one owner, add **'s** to the owner's name.

  Example: The <u>boy's</u> book | had some of <u>Pablo's</u> poems in it.

  one owner   one owner

- A noun that names two or more owners is plural and often ends in **–s**. If so, just add **'**.

  Example: The <u>boys'</u> teacher | read the two <u>poets'</u> poems out loud.

  more than one owner   more than one owner

A. Read each sentence. Circle the correct use of the possessive noun.

1. Pablo _____(Neruda's) / Nerudas'_____ home was in Chile.

2. _____ **Pablo's / Pablos'** _____ life was full of poetry.

3. The young _____ **boy's / boys'** _____ mind was full of creativity.

4. His father once asked who really wrote one _____ **poem's / poems'** _____ beautiful words.

5. At school the other _____ **student's / students'** _____ mean words did not stop him.

6. Pablo did not use his _____ **father's / fathers'** _____ last name.

7. He used his favorite _____ **poet's / poets'** _____ last name, Neruda.

8. Pablo Neruda did not like some of his _____ **government's / governments'** _____ actions.

9. He spoke for his _____ **reader's / readers'** _____ rights and the rights of all people.

10. You can still see many _____ **visitor's / visitors'** _____ notes on his fence.

Possessive Nouns, continued

B. Rewrite each sentence. Use a possessive noun in each sentence.

11. I like the poems of Gary Soto. _I like Gary Soto's poems._
_____

12. The ideas of the poet are so creative. _____
_____

13. The paintings of Diego Rivera showed the people of Mexico.
_____
_____

14. People still look at the works of this artist. _____
_____

15. The Vietnam Memorial has the names of many soldiers on it. _____
_____

16. Many veterans like the design of the memorial. _____
_____

17. The message of the wall is important. _____
_____

18. Maya Lin is well known for her public works. _____
_____

C. 19.–23. Edit the journal entry below. Make sure each possessive noun uses the apostrophe correctly.

Journal Entry

September 12, 1973

One of our countrys best poets died yesterday. I read many of this mans' poems.

The poets' words were so beautiful. I went to my friends' house. I wrote a message

on his fence. Many other admirer's messages are there, too. We will never forget

Neruda. His poems speak to everyone.

Revising and Editing Marks

∧	Add.
⟳	Move to here.
⟍	Replace with this.
℈	Take out.
⌃	Add a comma.
⊙	Add a period.
≡	Capitalize.
/	Make lower case.

Subjects and Predicates

Every sentence has two main parts. They are the **subject** and the **predicate**. There are different kinds of subjects and predicates.

> **Use Subjects and Predicates**
>
> • The subject tells whom or what the sentence is about. The **simple subject** is the most important word in the complete subject.
>
> • The predicate tells what the subject is, has, or does. The **simple predicate** is the verb.

Examples: The famous <u>poet</u>   <u>lived</u> in Chile.

                simple   simple
                subject   predicate

His <u>admirers</u>   still <u>write</u> messages on his fence.

        simple   simple
        subject   predicate

Today his <u>messages</u>   <u>are</u> still important.

        simple   simple
        subject   predicate

A. Circle the simple subject in each sentence. Underline the simple predicate.

1. Maya Lin's (memorial) <u>has</u> a strong message.

2. Her black granite wall tells us about the war.

3. Many people speak quietly near the wall.

4. The visitors remember the soldiers.

5. The wall honors Americans who died in the war.

6. The soldiers' lives were important to our country.

7. The public appreciates these heroes.

8. Maya Lin designs other monuments.

9. She is famous for her public works.

10. People leave flowers and candles at the wall.

Subjects and Predicates, continued

B. **Think about the poets Gary Soto and Pablo Neruda. Add a simple subject or a simple predicate to complete each sentence. Trade with a partner. Have your partner circle the simple subjects and underline the simple predicates.**

11. Both _____(poets)_____ share their

    thoughts with their readers.

12. Their _____ express

    their feelings and ideas about life.

13. Everyday _____ matter to both poets.

14. Their poems _____ messages across time.

15. Every word in their poems _____ important.

16. The readers _____ with the poets, too.

17. People in Chile still _____ messages on Pablo Neruda's gate.

18. Today _____ send e-mails or letters to Gary Soto.

19. The whole world _____ poets like Gary Soto and Pablo Neruda.

C. 20.–24. **Finish this letter to Maya Lin. Add subjects and predicates.**

February 18

Dear Maya Lin,

   Last week my family _____ . Your work

_____ . I _____ .

_____ feels so strong. The names on the wall

_____ . Thank you for making such a

special memorial for our soldiers. I will always remember my visit.

Yours truly,

Marita

Skills Review

A. Circle the complete subject in each sentence. Underline the complete predicate.

1. (In 1989, Maya Lin) created a civil rights memorial.

2. The Civil Rights Memorial is in Montgomery, Alabama.

3. The round black granite table tells the history of the Civil Rights Movement.

4. Clear water flows over the top of the table.

5. Dead heroes' names show under the water.

6. Thousands of visitors remember these heroes.

B. Read the passage. Underline all the nouns. Then write the nouns in the chart where they belong. Write each noun only once.

The Vietnam Veterans Memorial in Washington, D. C., is very popular. However, many people cannot travel to see it. John Devitt visited the memorial. He wanted people all over the United States to see this special black granite wall. John created The Moving Wall. This wall is much smaller than the original wall. It is a big success! Now it travels all over the country.

Soldiers who were in Vietnam built the wall. It went on display for the first time in Texas. Many volunteers are needed to set up the wall.

Common Nouns	Proper Nouns
7. people	14. Vietnam Veterans Memorial
8. _____	15. _____
9. _____	16. _____
10. _____	17. _____
11. _____	18. _____
12. _____	19. _____
13. _____	20. _____

Skills Review, continued

C. Write the correct singular or plural form for the word in parentheses.

21. Diego Rivera painted many big _____murals_____ in the 1930s. (**mural**)

22. Rivera was a very creative _____ . (**artist**)

23. He used many bright _____ like red, green, and yellow. (**color**)

24. He worked for many _____ on each mural. (**day**)

25. Some of his paintings show _____ working in the fields. (**woman**)

26. Other paintings show little Mexican _____ with big straw hats. (**child**)

27. Some of his paintings have mothers and _____ in them. (**baby**)

28. Many _____ admire Rivera's work. (**person**)

D. Rewrite each sentence. Use a possessive noun in each sentence.

29. The friend of the boy came to visit. _The boy's friend came to visit._____

_____

30. He brought some apples from the farm of his parents. _____

_____

31. The mother of the boy gave them some cookies. _____

_____

32. "We will put these on the desk of the teacher," they said. _____

_____

33. "They will be good for the lunches of the students." _____

_____

E. Add a simple subject or a simple predicate to complete each sentence.

34. Pablo Neruda _____wrote_____ many poems.

35. For many years, the _____ did not like his poems.

36. Chile's leaders did not _____ people near Neruda's home.

37. _____ went to Neruda's home anyway.

38. They _____ messages on his fence.

39. Now Neruda _____ a great hero in Chile.

Compound Sentences

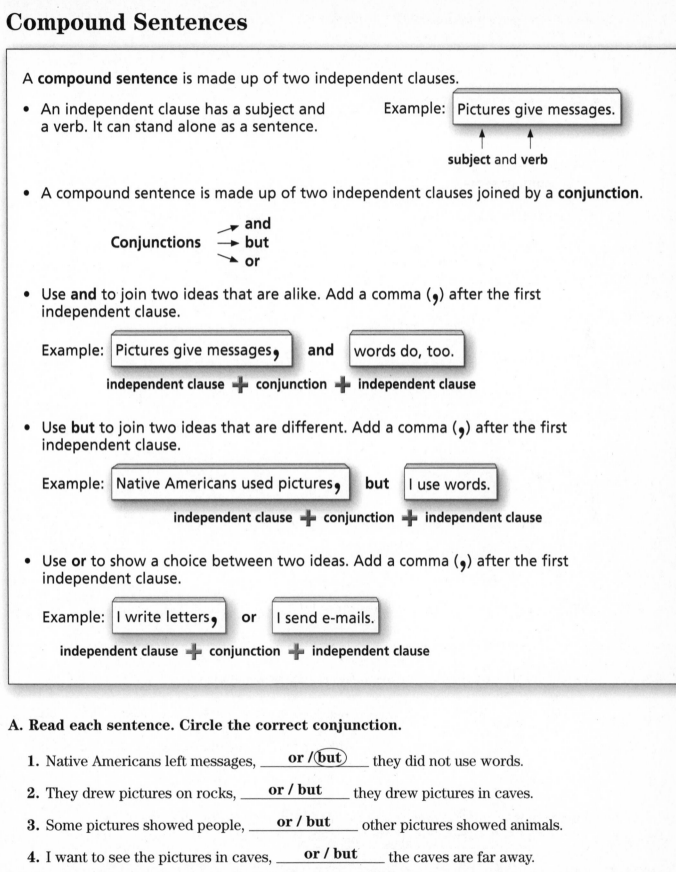

A **compound sentence** is made up of two independent clauses.

- An independent clause has a subject and a verb. It can stand alone as a sentence.

  Example: | Pictures give messages. |

  subject and **verb**

- A compound sentence is made up of two independent clauses joined by a **conjunction**.

  Conjunctions → **and**
  → **but**
  → **or**

- Use **and** to join two ideas that are alike. Add a comma (**,**) after the first independent clause.

  Example: | Pictures give messages**,** | **and** | words do, too. |

  independent clause ╋ conjunction ╋ independent clause

- Use **but** to join two ideas that are different. Add a comma (**,**) after the first independent clause.

  Example: | Native Americans used pictures**,** | **but** | I use words. |

  independent clause ╋ conjunction ╋ independent clause

- Use **or** to show a choice between two ideas. Add a comma (**,**) after the first independent clause.

  Example: | I write letters**,** | **or** | I send e-mails. |

  independent clause ╋ conjunction ╋ independent clause

A. Read each sentence. Circle the correct conjunction.

1. Native Americans left messages, _____ or /(but)_____ they did not use words.

2. They drew pictures on rocks, _____ or / but _____ they drew pictures in caves.

3. Some pictures showed people, _____ or / but _____ other pictures showed animals.

4. I want to see the pictures in caves, _____ or / but _____ the caves are far away.

5. I go to the library, _____ but / and _____ I borrow books about them.

Compound Sentences, continued

**B. Combine the sentences to make a compound sentence.
Use *and, but,* or *or*. Remember to add a comma.**

6. I read a poem about early Native American art. I liked it.

I read a poem about early Native American art, and I

liked it.

7. The poem did not say it was about messages. It was

about messages. _____

_____

8. It asked a question. I thought about the answer. _____

_____

9. Did the artists leave messages for other Native Americans? Did they leave messages for us?

_____

_____

10. The artists were in the canyon long ago. I am in the canyon now. _____

_____

11. I can't see the artists. I see their messages on the rocks. _____

_____

**C. Add an independent clause to make a compound sentence.
Remember to add a conjunction.**

I walked into the cave, _____and I saw pictures on the walls_____ . Some pictures
                                              12.

showed people, _____ . The pictures could be art,
                                    13.

_____ . Do the messages tell a story, _____
             14.

_____ ? I opened my notebook, _____
             15.

_____ . I like to look at pictures, _____
             16.

_____ !
             17.

**D. 18.–20. Tell a partner about the poem and pictures on page 38 of your book.
Use three compound sentences. Remember the conjunctions!**

Example: "I like the poem, but I like the picture better."

Articles

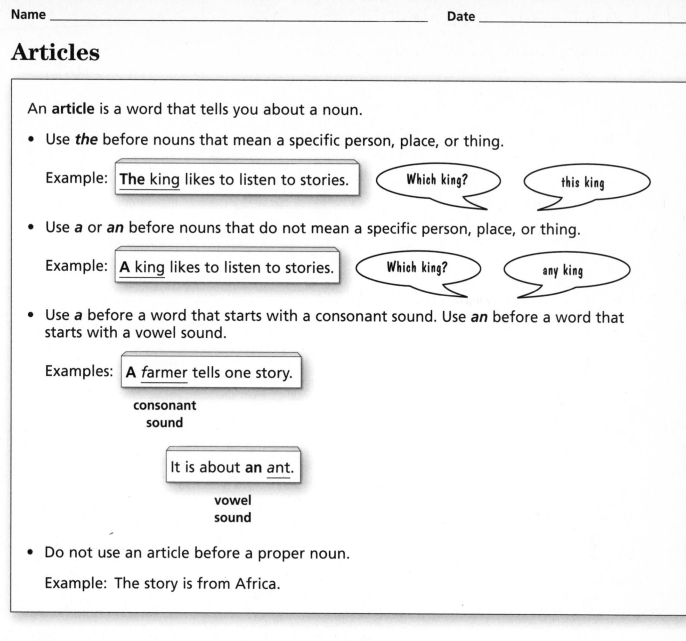

An **article** is a word that tells you about a noun.

- Use *the* before nouns that mean a specific person, place, or thing.

  Example: The king likes to listen to stories.

  Which king? *this king*

- Use *a* or *an* before nouns that do not mean a specific person, place, or thing.

  Example: A king likes to listen to stories.

  Which king? *any king*

- Use *a* before a word that starts with a consonant sound. Use *an* before a word that starts with a vowel sound.

  Examples: A farmer tells one story.

  consonant sound

  It is about an ant.

  vowel sound

- Do not use an article before a proper noun.

  Example: The story is from Africa.

A. Write *a, an,* or *the*. Use the clues in parentheses.

1. _____ A _____ king lived in Ethiopia. (**not specific**)

2. _____ king wanted to hear some stories. (**specific**)

3. He sent out _____ proclamation. (**not specific**)

4. He wanted _____ storytellers to tell stories until he cried, "Enough!" (**specific**)

5. A farmer had _____ idea. (**not specific**)

6. Her story did not have _____ end. (**not specific**)

7. It was about _____ wheat and some ants. (**specific**)

8. The farmer said over and over that _____ ant came and took another grain of wheat. (**not specific**)

Articles, continued

B. Write sentences about the picture. Use articles in the sentences. Use each article at least once.

"An owl took an oat..."

OAT

9. A lion was the king. _____

_____

10. _____

_____

11. _____

_____

12. _____

_____

13. _____

_____

14. _____

_____

C. 15.–27. Edit the journal entry below. Add the missing articles.

Journal Entry

My trip to Ethiopia is great. Today I heard storyteller tell story without end.

Story was interesting. It told about king who liked listening to stories. Farmer told

about granary. There was hole in it. Ant came and took out grain of wheat! Then

another ant came. Then another ant came. Finally king said, "Enough!" Farmer got half

of his kingdom. Now people in Ethiopia say, "One grain at a time brings good fortune."

Revising and Editing Marks

∧   Add.
    Move to here.
    Replace with this.
    Take out.
∧   Add a comma.
⊙   Add a period.
≡   Capitalize.
/   Make lower case.

© Hampton-Brown

Present Tense Verbs / Subject-Verb Agreement

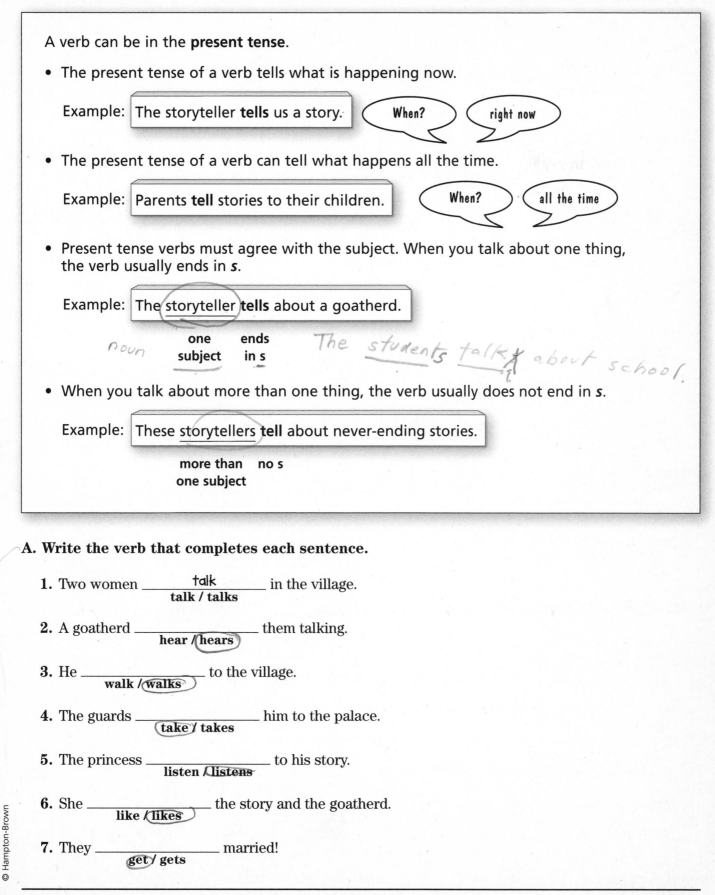

A verb can be in the **present tense**.

- The present tense of a verb tells what is happening now.

  Example: | The storyteller **tells** us a story. |

  When? *right now*

- The present tense of a verb can tell what happens all the time.

  Example: | Parents **tell** stories to their children. |

  When? *all the time*

- Present tense verbs must agree with the subject. When you talk about one thing, the verb usually ends in *s*.

  Example: | The storyteller **tells** about a goatherd. |

  noun   **one**   **ends**
            subject   **in s**

  The students talk about school.

- When you talk about more than one thing, the verb usually does not end in *s*.

  Example: | These storytellers **tell** about never-ending stories. |

  more than   no s
  one subject

A. Write the verb that completes each sentence.

1. Two women _____**talk**_____ in the village.
   talk / talks

2. A goatherd _____ them talking.
   hear / (hears)

3. He _____ to the village.
   walk / (walks)

4. The guards _____ him to the palace.
   (take) / takes

5. The princess _____ to his story.
   listen / (listens)

6. She _____ the story and the goatherd.
   like / (likes)

7. They _____ married!
   (get) / gets

Present Tense Verbs / Subject-Verb Agreement, continued

B. Write a verb to complete each sentence. Make the verb agree with the subject.

> **Verbs**
>
> agree   ~~eat~~   live   ~~tell~~   ~~stack~~   like
> ~~come~~   ~~harvest~~   invent   laugh   take   prove

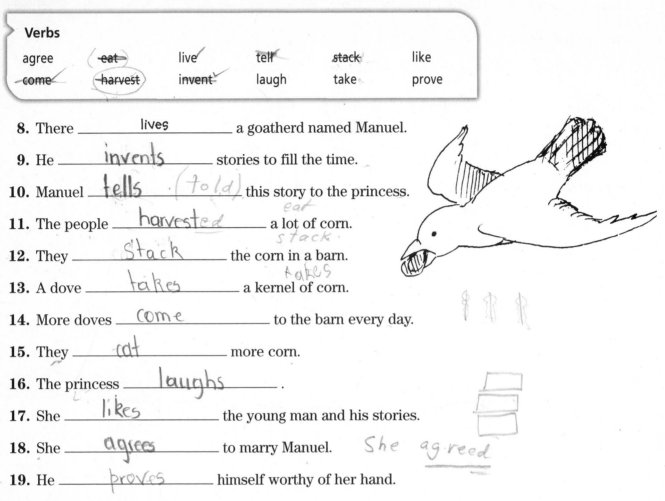

8. There _____lives_____ a goatherd named Manuel.

9. He _____invents_____ stories to fill the time.

10. Manuel _____tells____ (told) this story to the princess.

11. The people _____harvested_____ a lot of corn.

12. They _____stack_____ the corn in a barn.

13. A dove _____takes_____ a kernel of corn.

14. More doves _____come_____ to the barn every day.

15. They _____eat_____ more corn.

16. The princess _____laughs_____ .

17. She _____likes_____ the young man and his stories.

18. She _____agrees_____ to marry Manuel.   She agreed

19. He _____proves_____ himself worthy of her hand.

C. 20.–28. Edit the paragraph below. Make the verbs agree with the subjects.

> **Revising and Editing Marks**
>
> ∧   Add.
> ↻   Move to here.
> ⌄   Replace with this.
> ⌃   Take out.
> ∧̦   Add a comma.
> ⊙   Add a period.
> ≡   Capitalize.
> /   Make lower case.

Goatherds herds goats. They leads their goats to a meadow. The goats eat the grass. Sometimes a goatherd get lonely. "The Clever Goatherd" tells about a goatherd named Manuel. Manuel loves his goats. He feels lonely sometimes, though. He invents stories. The stories fills the time for him. One day Manuel decides not to be lonely anymore. He enters a contest. Manuel wins the contest! The goatherd proves, himself worthy of the princess's hand!

© Hampton-Brown

Nouns

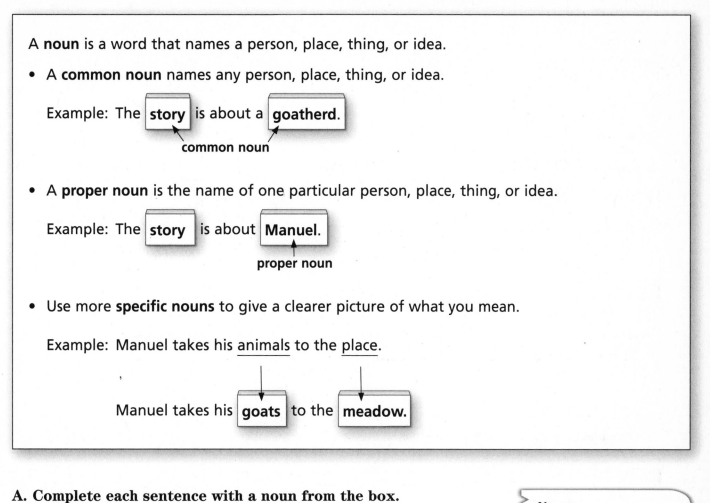

A **noun** is a word that names a person, place, thing, or idea.

- A **common noun** names any person, place, thing, or idea.

  Example: The | story | is about a | goatherd |.

  common noun

- A **proper noun** is the name of one particular person, place, thing, or idea.

  Example: The | story | is about | Manuel. |

  proper noun

- Use more **specific nouns** to give a clearer picture of what you mean.

  Example: Manuel takes his animals to the place.

  Manuel takes his | goats | to the | meadow. |

A. Complete each sentence with a noun from the box. Then circle all the proper nouns.

Nouns

Spain
end
stories
Margaret Lippert
princess
Manuel
goatherd
character

1. _____(Margaret Lippert)_____ is a storyteller.

2. She tells some never-ending _____ .

3. One of them is about a clever _____ .

4. It is a folk tale from _____ .

5. In it a _____ tells a story.

6. _____ keeps repeating the last line.

7. His story does not have an _____ .

8. The folk tale has an end when the _____ agrees to marry him!

Nouns, continued

B. 9.–15. Read the passage. Underline all the nouns. Then write the nouns in the chart where they belong. Give two examples of specific nouns.

I am writing about a clever frog. The character's name is Sam. This frog lives in Alabama, in a big pond called Frog Pond. I will repeat the last line of the story over and over again!

Common Nouns	Proper Nouns	Specific Nouns
frog	Sam	frog

C. Rewrite the sentences. Use a specific noun to replace the underlined noun.

16. Manuel herds his animals to the place. _Manuel herds his goats to the meadow._

_____

17. The villagers stack the stuff in a huge building. _____

_____

D. 18.–27. Edit the letter below to make it more specific. Change some common nouns to proper nouns or more specific nouns.

Dear Storyteller,

I like the story. I think the person is very clever. It is funny when the animal keeps taking the stuff. This story takes place in a country. Have you ever lived there? I would like to go visit. I could fly on a thing to get there. Maybe I could hear some other stories. Then I could write things, too. I would like to be a person like you!

Sincerely,

name

Revising and Editing Marks

∧	Add.
↶	Move to here.
⌇	Replace with this.
℘	Take out.
∧	Add a comma.
⊙	Add a period.
≡	Capitalize.
/	Make lower case.

Compound Sentences

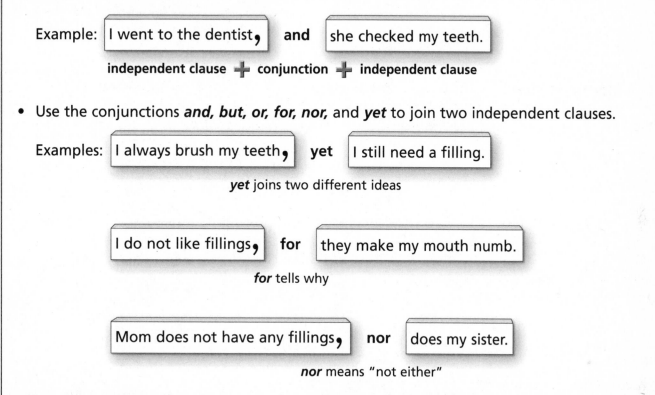

A **compound sentence** is made up of two independent clauses joined by a **conjunction**. Each independent clause has a subject and a verb.

Example: | I went to the dentist, | **and** | she checked my teeth. |

independent clause ➕ conjunction ➕ independent clause

- Use the conjunctions **and, but, or, for, nor**, and **yet** to join two independent clauses.

Examples: | I always brush my teeth, | **yet** | I still need a filling. |

yet joins two different ideas

| I do not like fillings, | **for** | they make my mouth numb. |

for tells why

| Mom does not have any fillings, | **nor** | does my sister. |

nor means "not either"

A. Write the conjunction that best completes each compound sentence.

1. I like to listen to the radio at night, _____but_____ I do not like to watch TV.
   but / nor

2. Sometimes I listen to music, _____ other times, I listen to a talk show.
   for / yet

3. Tonight the talk show is not about the news, _____ is it about a famous person.
   for / nor

4. It is about outer space, _____ it is very interesting.
   and / or

5. It is strange, _____ the man on it is from outer space.
   for / nor

6. The man is not from Earth, _____ he is not scary.
   but / nor

7. He says he likes pancakes, _____ he came to Earth to find them.
   and / or

8. Am I dreaming, _____ is this radio program real?
   but / or

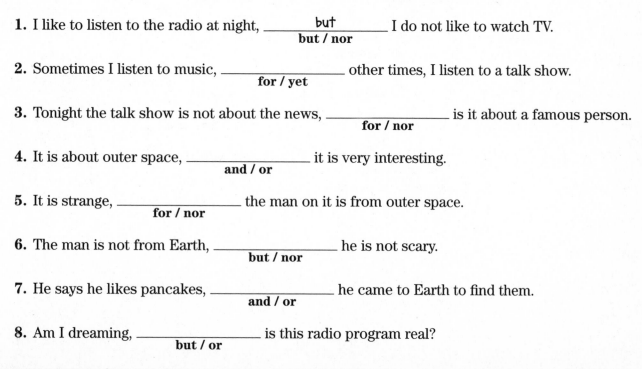

Compound Sentences, continued

B. Add an independent clause to make a compound sentence. Remember to use a conjunction.

Some Conjunctions	
and	for
but	not
or	yet

9. William gets a filling at the dentist,

   _____ and it is not too bad _____ .

10. It almost does not hurt,

   _____ .

11. William goes to bed,

   _____ .

12. He listens to a radio program,

   _____ .

13. Then William is surprised,

   _____ .

14. He is not imagining the show,

   _____ .

15. There is no radio,

   _____ .

16. The static was like music,

   _____ .

C. 17.–21. Edit the diary entry below. Combine sentences using conjunctions to create compound sentences.

Revising and Editing Marks

∧	Add.
↶	Move to here.
⌃	Replace with this.
୨	Take out.
⌄	Add a comma.
⊙	Add a period.
≡	Capitalize.
/	Make lower case.

Dear Diary,

   The strangest thing happened to me today. I was in bed. I was listening to a radio program. I was surprised. A man was riding in a flying saucer. He liked potato pancakes. There were no potato pancakes in space. People from outer space were coming to Earth. There are no real people from outer space. I was dreaming. I was imagining the whole thing.

William

Present Tense Verbs / Subject-Verb Agreement

The **verb** in a sentence must agree with its subject.

- A **singular subject** names one person, place, or thing. Use a **singular verb** with a singular subject.

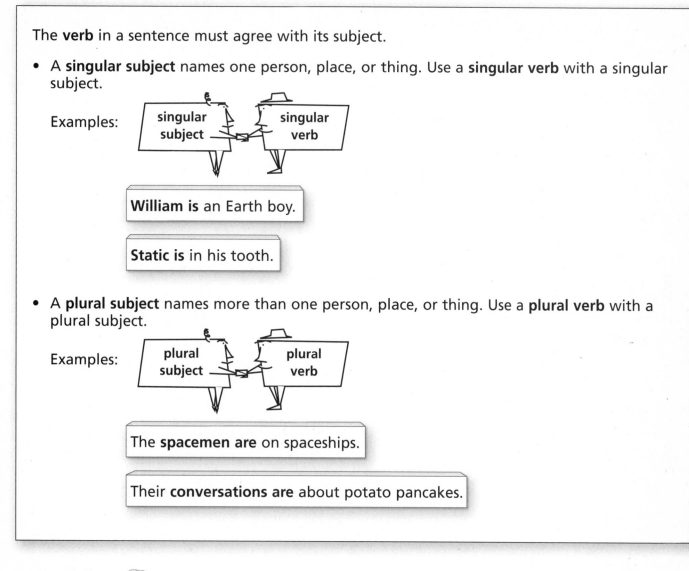

  Examples:

  singular subject — singular verb

  William is an Earth boy.

  Static is in his tooth.

- A **plural subject** names more than one person, place, or thing. Use a **plural verb** with a plural subject.

  Examples:

  plural subject — plural verb

  The **spacemen are** on spaceships.

  Their **conversations are** about potato pancakes.

A. Write *is* or *are* to complete each sentence.

1. The spacemen _____are_____ hungry.

2. They _____are_____ on Earth.

3. One spaceman _____is_____ in California.

4. He _____is_____ happy because he has a potato pancake to eat.

5. Yum! The potato pancake _____is_____ good.

6. Other fat men _____are_____ happy because they have junk food.

7. Junk food _____are_____ bad for them to eat.

8. It _____is_____ delicious, though!

Present Tense Verbs / Subject-Verb Agreement, continued

B. Circle the verb in each sentence. Then complete the sentence by writing a singular or plural subject that agrees with the verb.

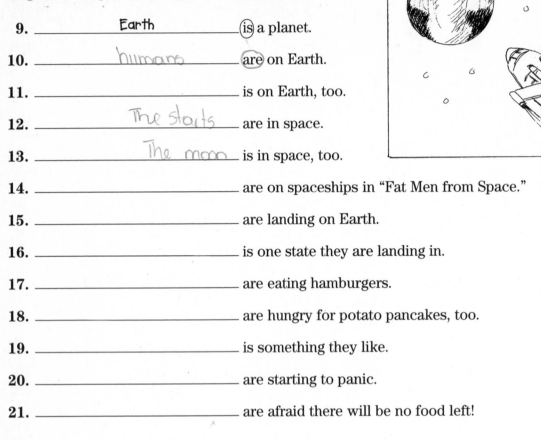

9. ____Earth____ (is) a planet.

10. ____humans____ (are) on Earth.

11. _____ is on Earth, too.

12. __The stars__ are in space.

13. __The moon__ is in space, too.

14. _____ are on spaceships in "Fat Men from Space."

15. _____ are landing on Earth.

16. _____ is one state they are landing in.

17. _____ are eating hamburgers.

18. _____ are hungry for potato pancakes, too.

19. _____ is something they like.

20. _____ are starting to panic.

21. _____ are afraid there will be no food left!

C. 22.–32. Edit the news story below. Add *is* and *are*.

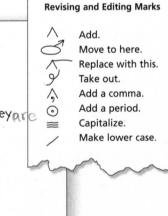

Revising and Editing Marks

∧ Add.
↷ Move to here.
⟋ Replace with this.
ℐ Take out.
⋏ Add a comma.
⊙ Add a period.
≡ Capitalize.
/ Make lower case.

Fat Men from Space

The reports ^are^ strange. Fat men ^are^ on Earth. Hundreds still in space! A spaceship ^is^ in the sky over me right now! The rumor that the fat men want potato pancakes. They ^are^ hungry for junk food, too. Earth people ^are^ scared. They ^are^ in a condition of panic. No junk food ^is^ left for them to eat! Now a giant potato pancake ^is^ in space. It ^is^ near the planet Ziegler. Stand by for more news.

Verbs

- An **action verb** tells what the subject does.

  Example: Daniel Manus Pinkwater, writes, books.
            subject   **action**
                                     verb

  What does Daniel do?

  He writes.

- A **linking verb** connects, or links, the subject to a word in the predicate. The word can describe the subject. The word can be another name for the subject.

  Examples: Daniel Manus Pinkwater, is, creative.
              subject   **linking**
                                       verb

  Daniel Manus Pinkwater, is, a writer.
             subject   **linking**
                                         verb

- A **verb** must agree with the subject. Use a **singular subject and singular verb** to tell about one person, place, or thing. Use a **plural subject and plural verb** to tell about more than one.

  Examples: Daniel Manus Pinkwater tells a story. It is amusing.

        singular subject ➕ **singular verb**

  Children enjoy Pinkwater's books. The books are wonderful!

    plural ➕ **plural**   **plural** ➕ **plural**
    subject   **verb**   **subject**   **verb**

A. Choose a verb from the box to complete each sentence. Then circle all the action verbs.

are ✓	play ✓
hears ✓	talk ✓
is ✓	works ✓

1. William's tooth _____is_____ a radio.

2. Radios ___play___ music, news, and conversations.

3. William ___hears___ static on his tooth sometimes.

4. The tooth ___works___ only at night.

5. The spacemen ___talk___ to each other at night.

6. They ___are___ quiet during the day.

Verbs, continued

B. Write a verb to complete each sentence. Use the type of verb that is named.

7. Fat men _____eat_____ a lot of junk food.
   <u>action verb</u>

8. Now sugar _____is_____ scarce.
   <u>linking verb</u>

9. William _____go_____ the dentist.
   <u>action verb</u>

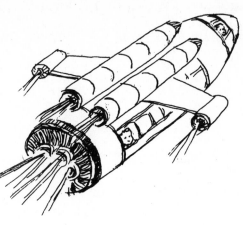

10. No cavities _____ in his teeth.
    <u>linking verb</u>

11. The radio _____ sometimes, though.
    <u>action verb</u>

12. William _____ the spacemen.
    <u>action verb</u>

13. The spacemen _____ in their spaceship.
    <u>action verb</u>

14. They _____ happy to be back in space.
    <u>linking verb</u>

15. They _____ the darkness of outer space.
    <u>action verb</u>

16. William _____ nothing on his teeth anymore.
    <u>action verb</u>

17. He often _____ the spacemen would come back.
    <u>action verb</u>

C. 18.–26. Edit the news story below. Make the verbs agree with the subjects.

	Revising and Editing Marks
∧	Add.
↰	Move to here.
⌃	Replace with this.
ϼ	Take out.
∧̂	Add a comma.
⊙	Add a period.
≡	Capitalize.
/	Make lower case.

Daniel Manus Pinkwater

Daniel Manus Pinkwater are an author. He write books for children. Children loves his books. The stories is funny. Sometimes they is weird, too. Pinkwater remember his childhood. He gets some ideas from it. Then he put those ideas in his books. His messages is good for young people. They likes the messages and the books!

Skills Review

A. Combine the sentences to make a compound sentence. Use the correct conjunction from the parentheses.

1. We read two tales. They both had never-ending stories in them. (**and, or**) _____

   We read two tales, and they both had never-ending stories in them.

2. One tale is set in Ethiopia. The other is set in Spain. (**nor, but**) _____

   _____

3. I like the tale about the farmer. My friend likes the tale about the goatherd. (**yet, for**)

   _____

4. The farmer is clever. The ending of her story keeps repeating. (**nor, for**) _____

   _____

5. The goatherd is also clever. The princess decides to marry him. (**and, or**) _____

   _____

6. She thinks his stories are funny. They make her smile. (**and, or**) _____

   _____

7. She tells him he proved himself. She will marry him. (**and, or**) _____

   _____

8. The goatherd might marry the princess. He might go back to his goats. (**nor, or**) _____

   _____

B. Write *a*, *an*, or *the* to complete each sentence. Use the clue in parentheses.

9. A story has a beginning, a middle, and _____an_____ end. (**not specific**)

10. _____ author introduces characters at the beginning. (**specific**)

11. The king is _____ character in "The Storyteller." (**not specific**)

12. _____ setting of this story is Ethiopia. (**specific**)

13. This story has _____ story inside it. (**not specific**)

14. That story is about _____ ant. (**not specific**)

15. _____ ant takes some wheat. (**specific**)

16. "The Storyteller" ends when _____ king says, "Enough." (**specific**)

C. Choose the verb that correctly completes each sentence.

17. Manuel _____lives_____ in Spain.
   live / lives

18. Spain _____ a country in Europe.
   is / are

19. Manuel _____ goats.
   herd / herds

20. Goats _____ animals.
   is / are

21. They _____ grass.
   eat / eats

22. Grass _____ in meadows.
   grow / grows

23. Many goatherds _____ their goats to the meadow outside of the village.
   take / takes

D. Complete each sentence with a noun from the box. Then circle all the proper nouns in the sentences.

Nouns	
Earth	September
radio	year
teeth	filling
Dr. Greene	

24. _____(Dr. Greene)_____ is a dentist.

25. I visit him every _____ in March.

26. Then I go again in the month of _____ ,

27. The dentist checks my _____ for cavities.

28. Once I was like William, and I needed a _____ .

29. There was no _____ in my filling.

30. I did not hear conversations of spacemen on _____ .

E. Write a verb to complete each sentence. Use the type of verb that is named. Make sure the verb agrees with the subject.

31. "Fat Men from Space" _____is_____ science fiction.
   linking verb

32. The author _____ about some real things.
   action verb

33. Dentists _____ real people.
   linking verb

34. People _____ junk food.
   action verb

35. Spacemen _____ not real.
   linking verb

Skills Review and Practice Tests

A. Circle the complete subject in each sentence. Underline the complete predicate.

1. Messages matter.

2. People send messages to communicate ideas.

3. Gary Soto writes messages in poems.

4. Diego Rivera painted messages in murals.

5. Maya Lin uses monuments and memorials for messages.

6. Many people wrote messages on Pablo Neruda's fence.

7. Authors share messages in their stories.

8. You and I send messages, too.

9. We communicate our messages in many ways.

10. I like to send messages by e-mail.

B. Use the subject or predicate to write a complete sentence. Tell about messages.

11. people _People send messages every day._____

_____

12. talk on the telephone _____

_____

13. use their computer _____

_____

14. the message in the story _____

_____

15. some artists _____

_____

16. listen to the messages in songs _____

_____

**C. Read the passage. Read each item carefully. Choose the best answer.
Mark your answer.**

Maya Lin is an architect. <u>Is a sculptor, too.</u> Maya Lin wants her work to send messages to

people. <u>Her buildings, monuments, and sculptures.</u>

               2

Maya Lin was born in 1959. <u>She grew up in Ohio.</u> She liked to play in the woods. The

                                       3

importance of nature is one of the messages that Maya Lin shares in her work.

Maya Lin went to college at Yale University. She designed the Vietnam Veterans Memorial when

she was a student there. <u>Messages about the Vietnam War from the memorial.</u>

                                                4

Maya Lin designed the Civil Rights Memorial. The message was about freedom. She wanted to

tell a story about the people who worked hard to change laws so all Americans would be treated

fairly. The memorial gives visitors a message about civil rights.

Maya Lin designed a sculpture at Yale University. It gives a message about women students

there. Wave Field is another sculpture. It gives a message about nature. Maya Lin lives in New York

City. <u>She still.</u>

5

---

17. In number 1, <u>Is a sculptor, too</u> is best written —
- Ⓐ She a sculptor, too.
- Ⓑ She is a sculptor, too.
- Ⓒ A sculptor, too.
- Ⓓ as it is written

18. In number 2, <u>Her buildings, monuments, and
sculptures</u> is best written —
- Ⓕ Her buildings, monuments, and sculptures are.
- Ⓖ Are her buildings monuments, and sculptures.
- Ⓗ Her buildings, monuments, and sculptures send the messages.
- Ⓙ as it is written

19. In number 3, <u>She grew up in Ohio</u> is best
written —
- Ⓐ adding a complete subject
- Ⓑ adding a complete predicate
- Ⓒ adding a complete subject and predicate
- Ⓓ as it is written

20. In number 4, <u>Messages about the Vietnam War
from the memorial</u> is best written —
- Ⓕ Visitors get messages about the Vietnam War from the memorial.
- Ⓖ Messages about the Vietnam War from the memorial are.
- Ⓗ People messages about the Vietnam War from the memorial.
- Ⓙ as it is written

21. In number 5, <u>She still</u> is best written —
- Ⓐ Still shares her messages through her work.
- Ⓑ Her messages through her work.
- Ⓒ She still shares her messages through her work.
- Ⓓ as it is written

Skills Review and Practice Tests, continued

D. Combine the sentences to make a compound sentence.

22. People could not always travel in space. They can now.

_____

_____

23. They travel in space. They send back messages.

_____

_____

24. The messages can be words. The messages can be pictures.

_____

_____

25. The messages are important. People on Earth learn about space from them.

_____

_____

26. There is a space station in space. Astronauts live in it.

_____

_____

27. They are living in space. They can still send back messages!

_____

_____

E. 28.–35. Write the verb that correctly completes each sentence.

It _____is_____ July 20, 1969. The first people _____ on the moon. They
    is / are   **land / lands**

_____ astronauts. Neil Armstrong _____ on the moon first. He
  is / are   **step / steps**

_____ footprints. The footprints _____ still there. The astronauts
 leave / leaves   **is / are**

_____ a U.S. flag on the moon. The flag _____ a message in space!
 plant / plants   **is / are**

Skills Review and Practice Tests, continued

F. Read the passage. Read each item carefully. Choose the best answer. Mark your answer.

In "Fat Men from Space," spacemen visit Earth. William hears their messages. His tooth is like a radio. <u>The story is make-believe. There are no real spacemen</u>. Spacemen do not really send
1
messages to Earth!

There are real people in space, <u>nor</u> those people do send messages to Earth! Alan Shepard
2
went into space in 1961. <u>He was the first American in space. He only stayed up for 15 minutes</u>.
3
In 1962, John Glenn orbited Earth. In 1969, Neil Armstrong walked on the moon. He sent a message back to Earth. He said, "That's one small step for man, one giant leap for mankind."

Some spacecraft go into space without people in them. They <u>takes</u> pictures of planets. Then
4
they send the pictures back to Earth. The pictures <u>are</u> messages. Each message gives information
5
about space. Now there is a space station in space. It <u>orbit</u> Earth.
6

---

36. The best way to combine the sentences in number 1 is —

Ⓐ The story is make-believe, or there are no real spacemen.

Ⓑ The story is make-believe, for there are no real spacemen.

Ⓒ The story is make-believe, yet there are no real spacemen.

Ⓓ The sentences cannot be combined.

37. In number 2, the conjunction should be —

Ⓕ and

Ⓖ or

Ⓗ for

Ⓙ as it is written

38. The best way to combine the sentences in number 3 is —

Ⓐ He was the first American in space, nor he only stayed up for 15 minutes.

Ⓑ He was the first American in space, for he only stayed up for 15 minutes.

Ⓒ He was the first American in space, but he only stayed up for 15 minutes.

Ⓓ The sentences cannot be combined.

39. In number 4, the action verb should be —

Ⓕ are

Ⓖ is

Ⓗ take

Ⓙ as it is written

40. In number 5, the linking verb should be —

Ⓐ is

Ⓑ shows

Ⓒ show

Ⓓ as it is written

41. In number 6, the action verb should be —

Ⓕ orbits

Ⓖ is

Ⓗ are

Ⓙ as it is written

36

Present and Past Tense Verbs

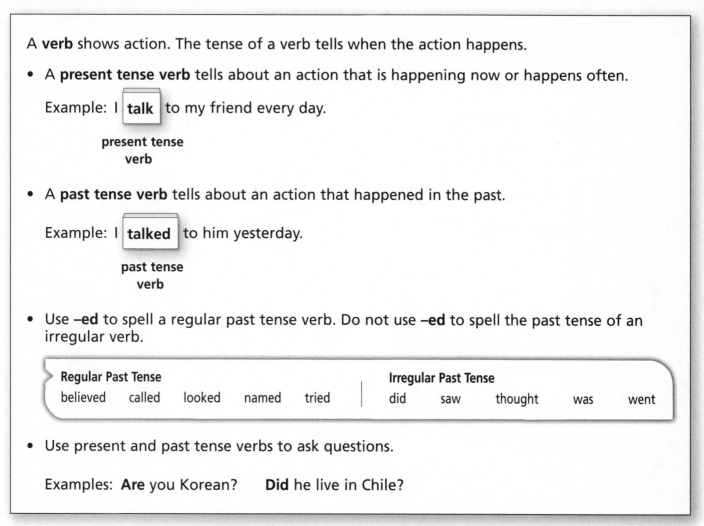

A **verb** shows action. The tense of a verb tells when the action happens.

- A **present tense verb** tells about an action that is happening now or happens often.

  Example: I │ **talk** │ to my friend every day.

  present tense
  verb

- A **past tense verb** tells about an action that happened in the past.

  Example: I │ **talked** │ to him yesterday.

  past tense
  verb

- Use **–ed** to spell a regular past tense verb. Do not use **–ed** to spell the past tense of an irregular verb.

Regular Past Tense					Irregular Past Tense				
believed	called	looked	named	tried	did	saw	thought	was	went

- Use present and past tense verbs to ask questions.

  Examples: **Are** you Korean?   **Did** he live in Chile?

A. Read each sentence. Circle the correct present or past tense verb.

1. These days my grandmother _____ (visits)/ visited _____ us every week.

2. She _____ lived / lives _____ in Korea when she was a girl.

3. Every week she _____ tells / told _____ stories about the old country.

4. Her family _____ move / moved _____ to Chicago when she was ten years old.

5. She _____ brings / brought _____ some of her Korean storybooks with her.

6. She _____ gives / gave _____ one of her books to me!

7. She still _____ spoke / speaks _____ Korean.

8. I always _____ listened / listen _____ to her carefully.

9. Now I _____ say / said _____ many Korean words to her.

Present and Past Tense Verbs, continued

B. Write the correct verb from the box to complete each sentence.

<table>
<tr><td colspan="3">**Some Present and Past Tense Verbs**</td></tr>
<tr><td colspan="2">**Present Tense Verbs**</td><td>**Past Tense Verbs**</td></tr>
<tr><td>run</td><td>am</td><td>kicked   played</td></tr>
<tr><td>go</td><td>play</td><td>won   cheered</td></tr>
<tr><td></td><td></td><td>went   thought</td></tr>
<tr><td></td><td></td><td>was</td></tr>
</table>

10. I _____ go _____ to school every weekday.

11. I also _____ to soccer practice yesterday.

12. I _____ a busy person!

13. On Monday afternoons, I _____ soccer.

14. I _____ three miles at each practice.

15. Last week my team _____ to another school.

16. We _____ against their best team.

17. The crowd _____ each goal.

18. I _____ we might lose.

19. I _____ the last goal.

20. My team _____ the game.

21. I _____ very happy!

C. Complete the sentences. Trade with a partner. Have your partner circle the present tense verbs and underline the past tense verbs.

22. My favorite activity _____ (is) reading stories _____ .

23. My favorite character _____ .

24. He _____ .

25. One time this character _____ .

26. In another book, he _____ .

27. I really like it when he _____ .

D. 28.–30. Tell a partner about your favorite singer or music. Use present tense verbs. Tell about a singer or music you liked when you were younger. Use past tense verbs.

Example: "When I was four, I listened to nursery rhymes. Now I like rock music."

Past Tense Verbs

A **past tense verb** shows that an action happened before, or in the past.

- The past tense of regular verbs ends with **–ed**. Use these rules to form the past tense.

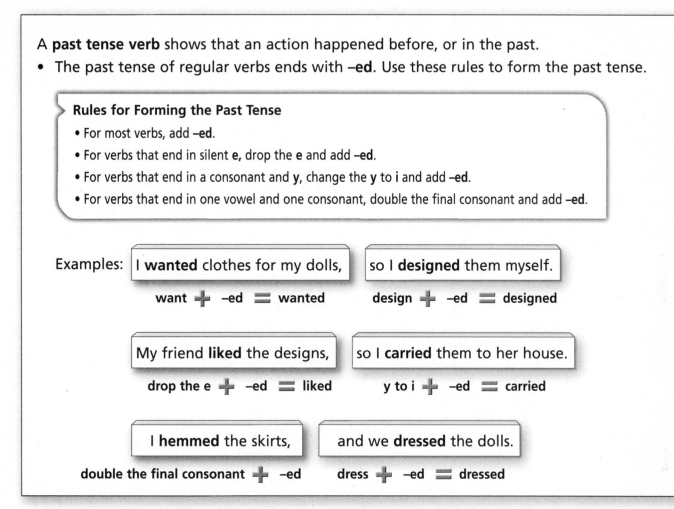

Rules for Forming the Past Tense

- For most verbs, add **–ed**.
- For verbs that end in silent **e**, drop the **e** and add **–ed**.
- For verbs that end in a consonant and **y**, change the **y** to **i** and add **–ed**.
- For verbs that end in one vowel and one consonant, double the final consonant and add **–ed**.

Examples:

| I **wanted** clothes for my dolls, | so I **designed** them myself. |

want **+** –ed **=** wanted   design **+** –ed **=** designed

| My friend **liked** the designs, | so I **carried** them to her house. |

drop the e **+** –ed **=** liked   y to i **+** –ed **=** carried

| I **hemmed** the skirts, | and we **dressed** the dolls. |

double the final consonant **+** –ed   dress **+** –ed **=** dressed

A. Write the past tense for the verb in parentheses.

1. My family _____ moved _____ to Los Angeles last year. (**move**)

2. One day Mom and I _____ a quilting class. (**join**)

3. We _____ to the library for the class. (**walk**)

4. The teacher _____ us what to do. (**show**)

5. We _____ every pattern. (**try**)

6. We _____ lots of pretty colors in our quilts. (**use**)

7. We _____ several quilts. (**finish**)

8. We _____ everyone to the class quilt show. (**invite**)

9. They _____ our quilts! (**like**)

10. We _____ many quilts as gifts. (**wrap**)

B. 11.–21. Read the story. Then rewrite the story. Change the underlined verbs to the past tense.

Quilting with Aunt Rosa

I <u>help</u> my Aunt Rosa make quilts. First we <u>look</u> in quilt books for a good design. Next we <u>use</u> paper and pencils to draw the design. After that we <u>decide</u> on the colors. Then we <u>shop</u> for the cloth. We <u>carry</u> the cloth home in a big paper bag. Aunt Rosa and I <u>sew</u> all weekend. We <u>talk</u> and <u>laugh</u>, too. On Sunday night, we <u>admire</u> our new quilt. I <u>clap</u> my hands with joy at our work.

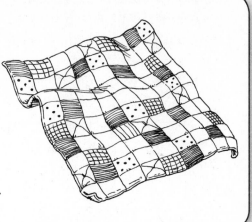

I <u>helped</u> my Aunt Rosa make quilts.

_____

_____

_____

_____

_____

_____

C. 22.–27. Edit the letter below. Use the correct form of the past tense for each verb.

Revising and Editing Marks

∧   Add.
◯ↄ   Move to here.
∧   Replace with this.
ℊ   Take out.
∧⌣   Add a comma.
⊙   Add a period.
≡   Capitalize.
╱   Make lower case.

April 24

Dear Mom,

    Yesterday I receive the big box of old scraps. Thanks a lot! When I open the

box, the cats jump right in. They drag scraps from my old blue dress onto the floor.

Then they wrap themselves up in scraps from my green shirt. The cats pick the

scraps for my next quilt!

Love,

Narin

© Hampton-Brown

Irregular Past Tense Verbs

Irregular verbs have special forms to show the past tense.

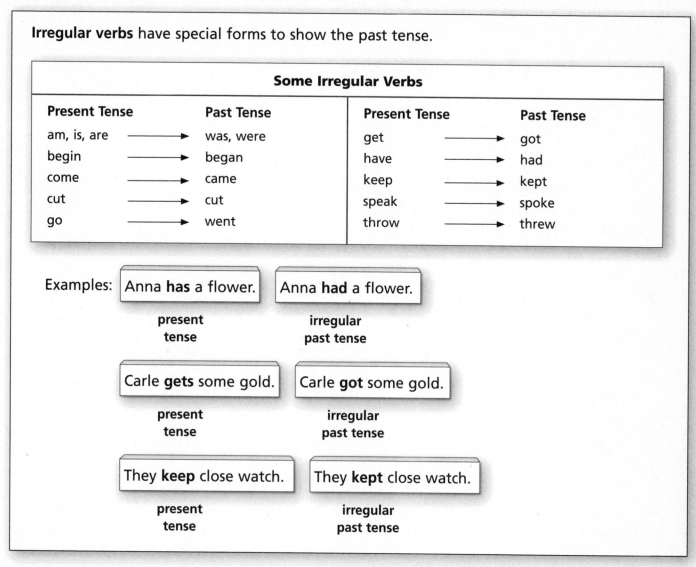

Some Irregular Verbs			
Present Tense	**Past Tense**	**Present Tense**	**Past Tense**
am, is, are ⟶	was, were	get ⟶	got
begin ⟶	began	have ⟶	had
come ⟶	came	keep ⟶	kept
cut ⟶	cut	speak ⟶	spoke
go ⟶	went	throw ⟶	threw

Examples:

Anna **has** a flower.	Anna **had** a flower.
present tense	irregular past tense

Carle **gets** some gold.	Carle **got** some gold.
present tense	irregular past tense

They **keep** close watch.	They **kept** close watch.
present tense	irregular past tense

A. Read each present tense verb. Draw a line to its irregular past tense form.

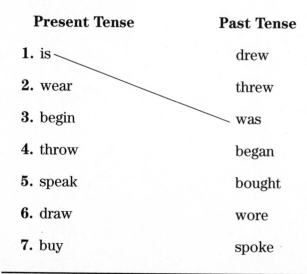

Present Tense	Past Tense
1. is	drew
2. wear	threw
3. begin	was
4. throw	began
5. speak	bought
6. draw	wore
7. buy	spoke

Irregular Past Tense Verbs, continued

B. 8.–28. Read the story about quilting. Then rewrite the story. Change the underlined verbs to the past tense form. Be sure to spell irregular verbs correctly.

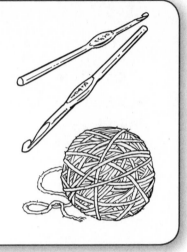

A Fun Family Tradition

Grandma Bess <u>learns</u> crochet from her mother, Marie. It <u>is</u> a family tradition. Grandma Bess <u>teaches</u> my mom when my mom <u>is</u> a girl. My mom and grandma <u>teach</u> me.

We <u>have</u> fun. Grandma <u>comes</u> to my house every Friday. She <u>brings</u> her needles and yarn. "Make your pattern carefully," they <u>tell</u> me. I <u>try</u>. I <u>make</u> one piece at a time. Time <u>flies</u>. It <u>gets</u> late before we <u>know</u> it. Finally I <u>do</u> it! I finish my first crochet. I <u>think</u> it <u>is</u> a sweater, but it only <u>has</u> one arm! We <u>laugh</u> and <u>laugh</u>.

Grandma Bess <u>learned</u> crochet from her mother, Marie.

_____

_____

_____

_____

_____

C. 29.–36. Edit the letter below. Use the correct form of the irregular past tense for each verb.

Revising and Editing Marks

∧	Add.
⟳	Move to here.
⋏	Replace with this.
ꝯ	Take out.
⌄	Add a comma.
⊙	Add a period.
≡	Capitalize.
/	Make lower case.

April 30

Dear Narin,

I get your letter. Thanks for the good advice! Last week your aunt Tina and I mades a new quilt for Ester's baby. We buy red, blue, yellow, and green cloth. We cut it up into small squares. We put the squares together. We bind it with gold cloth. Then we take it to Ester's house. She is so surprised! She lay it on the baby's bed right away. She take a picture, too.

Love,

Mom

© Hampton-Brown

Future Tense Verbs

A **future tense verb** tells what will happen later, or in the future.

- Use the helping verbs **will, is going to,** or **are going to** plus a main verb to form the future tense.

Some Future Tense Verbs

Verbs with Will	Verbs with Is / Are Going To
will move	is going to move, are going to move
will sew	is going to sew, are going to sew
will tell	is going to tell, are going to tell

Examples: I **will** **make** another quilt next week.

helping + main
verb   verb

Lara **is going to** **help** me.

helping + main
verb   verb

We **are going to** **sew** carefully.

helping + main
verb   verb

A. Write a future form of the verb in parentheses.

1. Grandma _____is going to have_____ a birthday soon. (**have**)

2. There _____ a big family party. (**be**)

3. Uncle Roberto _____ a special cake. (**bake**)

4. Aunt Amelia _____ the house with beautiful flowers. (**decorate**)

5. The grandchildren _____ a quilt. (**make**)

6. We _____ special paint on our hands. (**put**)

7. Then we _____ our hands onto a big piece of cloth. (**press**)

Future Tense Verbs, continued

B. Rewrite each sentence. Use the future tense.

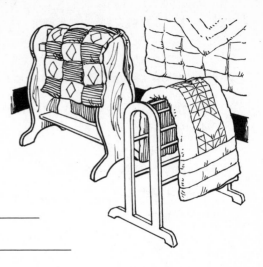

8. There is a new store at the mall. There will be a new store at the mall. / There is going to be a new store at the mall.

9. The store sells quilts from all over the world. _____

10. My mom goes to the store. _____

11. She buys a wedding present for my sister. _____

12. Mom gives the quilt to my sister. _____

13. My sister loves the quilt. _____

C. 14.–24. Edit the journal entry below. Use the future tense for each verb.

Journal Entry

May 9

My grandfather makes animal quilts for all of the grandchildren. Everyone helps him. We pick out our favorite colors of cloth. I choose the cloth with blue flowers. My brother, Stan, draws the animal patterns on paper. My cousin, Frieda, cuts out the animals. Little Tom hands them to Grandfather. I thread the needles for him. Grandfather works for a long time. He finishes all of the quilts. The grandchildren are so excited!

Revising and Editing Marks

∧	Add.
⌒	Move to here.
⌒	Replace with this.
℈	Take out.
∧	Add a comma.
⊙	Add a period.
≡	Capitalize.
/	Make lower case.

© Hampton-Brown

Verb Tense

The **tense** of a verb shows **when** an action happens.

- The **present tense** shows that the action happens now.
- The **past tense** shows that the action happened in the past.
- The **future tense** shows that the action will happen later.

Earlier	Now	Later
Past Tense	Present Tense	Future Tense
grew	grow	will grow, is going to grow
promised	promise	will promise, is going to promise
wrapped	wrap	will wrap, is going to wrap

Tense	Examples	
present tense	Patricia Polacco **writes** books.	They **write** books, too.
past tense	She **wrote** a story about a quilt.	They **wrote** about traditions.
future tense	She **will write** more stories.	They **are going to write** more stories, too.

A. Read each sentence. Circle the correct verb to complete each sentence.

1. Right now I _____ (**have**) / **had** / **will have** _____ a little red wooden horse.

2. My grandfather _____ **bring / brought / is going to bring** _____ it from Sweden in 1940.

3. He _____ **give / gave / will give** _____ it to my grandmother as a wedding gift fifty years ago.

4. Then the horse _____ **sits / sat / is going to sit** _____ on a bookcase in their home.

5. A few years ago, my grandmother _____ **gives / gave / will give** _____ me the horse.

6. I _____ **thank / thanked / am going to thank** _____ her with a big hug right away.

7. Now the horse _____ **is / was / will be** _____ on my desk.

8. It _____ **reminds / reminded / is going to remind** me of my grandparents.

9. Some day I _____ **have / had / will have** _____ children.

10. Then I _____ **give / gave / will give** _____ the special horse to them.

Verb Tense, continued

B. Write sentences of your own. Tell about a special gift. Use verbs in the past, present, and future tenses.

11. Past Tense: _____

_____

_____

12. Present Tense: _____

_____

_____

13. Future Tense: _____

_____

_____

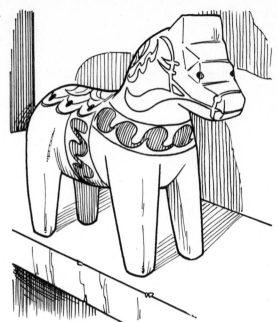

14. Past Tense: _____

_____

15. Present Tense: _____

_____

16. Future Tense: _____

_____

C. 17.–24. A reader might write this letter to the author. Edit the letter. Use the correct form of the verb in each sentence.

March 18

Dear Ms. Polacco,

   Last week I reads your book about the keeping quilt. I will like the story a lot.

I am going to see the characters in my mind. Yesterday I tell my friend about the

book. She want the book, too. Tomorrow I took the book to her. Then we talks about

the book. Next week we read another one of your books.

Sincerely,

Hilda

Revising and Editing Marks

∧   Add.
↰   Move to here.
⌃   Replace with this.
ℐ   Take out.
⌃,   Add a comma.
⊙   Add a period.
≡   Capitalize.
/   Make lower case.

46

Questions

When you want information, you ask a **question**.

- Use **question words** to ask a question. End your question with a question mark.

Question Words		
Can Do, Does, Did Am, Is, Are	How What When	Where Who Why

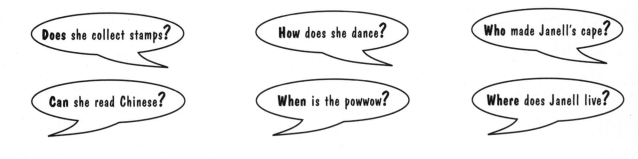

- You can also form questions with a tag at the end.

  Examples: Janell has an Indian name, **doesn't she**?

  She can fish, **can't she**?

A. Read each question. Circle the correct question word.

1. _____Where / (What)_____ is on Janell's cape and shawl?

2. _____How / Why_____ long has Janell been dancing?

3. _____Is / Can_____ Janell do beadwork?

4. _____Are / Who_____ made young Janell's outfits?

5. _____When / Am_____ does Janell want to do more beadwork?

6. _____What / Is_____ Guangdong, China, close to Hong Kong?

7. _____Who / Where_____ does Jenny like to curl up?

8. _____Where / Why_____ does Yingyi use the name "Jenny"?

9. _____Does / Am_____ Jenny respect other people's rights?

10. _____Can / Are_____ Jenny and Janell interesting people?

Questions, continued

B. Read the statements about Janell and Jenny. Turn the statements into questions. Use question words.

Statements	Questions
11. Janell likes to dance.	Who likes to dance?
12. Jenny reads mysteries.	
13. Janell is a Native American.	
14. Jenny lived in China.	
15. Janell lives on a reservation.	
16. Some people teased Jenny.	

C. 17.–23. Edit the interview questions below. Make sure the tag questions are correct.

Interview

You speak both Spanish and English, wasn't you?

You used to live in Peru, isn't you?

You are the oldest child in your family, don't you?

You were just on vacation in Texas, didn't you?

Your father has a band, won't he?

Your sister is a singer, aren't she?

You will learn to play the drums soon, isn't you?

Revising and Editing Marks

∧	Add.
↶	Move to here.
⌃	Replace with this.
୨	Take out.
⌄	Add a comma.
⊙	Add a period.
≡	Capitalize.
/	Make lower case.

Transitive and Intransitive Verbs

A **transitive verb** needs an object to complete its meaning.
- The object answers the question **Whom?** or **What?**

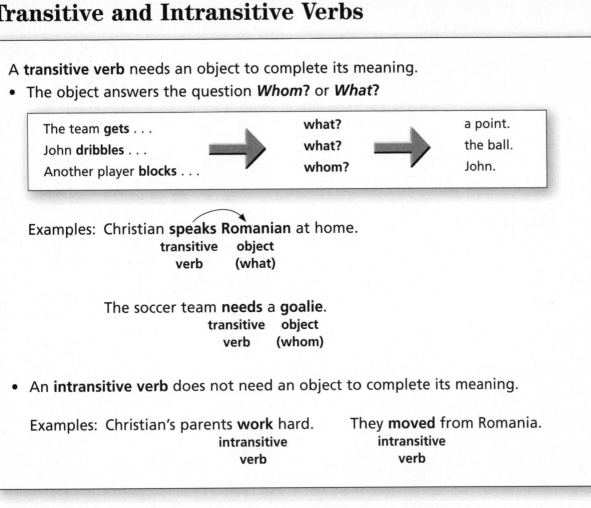

The team **gets** . . .	what?	a point.
John **dribbles** . . .	what?	the ball.
Another player **blocks** . . .	whom?	John.

Examples: Christian **speaks Romanian** at home.
             transitive   object
             verb   (what)

The soccer team **needs** a **goalie**.
          transitive   object
          verb   (whom)

- An **intransitive verb** does not need an object to complete its meaning.

Examples: Christian's parents **work** hard.   They **moved** from Romania.
                intransitive   intransitive
                verb   verb

A. Clara had an experience like Christian's. Circle the verb in each sentence. Underline the object if there is one. Write if the verb is transitive or intransitive.

1. Clara (lived) in Puerto Rico. _____

2. She moved to Philadelphia at age ten. _____

3. Clara's parents bought a house in a pretty neighborhood. _____

4. Soon Clara made many friends. _____

5. Clara learned English quickly. _____

6. Her parents adjusted slowly. _____

7. One day Clara shared her culture with the class. _____

8. Her father played his guitar. _____

9. Her mother told stories. _____

10. Then her parents felt happy in this country. _____

Transitive and Intransitive Verbs, continued

B. Complete the sentence. Use either a transitive or an intransitive verb as shown.

11. Christian's family came _____to the United States_____ .
intransitive

12. Christian keeps _____ .
transitive

13. He goes _____ .
intransitive

14. Christian takes _____ .
transitive

15. He writes _____ .
transitive

16. The family left _____ .
transitive

17. They moved _____ .
intransitive

18. They adjusted _____ .
intransitive

19. Sometimes they still communicate _____ .
intransitive

20. Christian loves _____ .
transitive

C. Think about "Beyond the Color Lines." Complete the sentences. Trade with a partner. Have your partner circle the verbs and write "transitive" or "intransitive" to describe them. Have your partner underline the objects of transitive verbs.

21. Janell (enjoys) _____Native American traditions_____ .   transitive

22. Janell dances _____ .   _____

23. Janell likes _____ .   _____

24. She answers _____ .   _____

25. Jenny reads _____ .   _____

26. Jenny feels _____ .   _____

27. As a young girl, Jenny lived _____ .   _____

28. Christian writes _____ .   _____

29. In his senior year, Christian will attend _____ .   _____

30. All three students speak _____ .   _____

Helping Verbs

Some verbs have more than one word. The last word is the main verb. The verb that comes before it is the **helping verb**.

> **Some Helping Verbs**
> can   could   may   might   must   would   should

- The helping verb adds information to the main verb. The helping verb agrees with the subject.

    Examples: Janell [can] [go] to a powwow.
    helping + main
    verb   verb

    Jenny [might] [learn] to read Chinese one day.
    helping + main
    verb   verb

    Christian [should] [write] more poetry.
    helping + main
    verb   verb

A. Choose a helping verb from the box to complete each sentence. You may use some helping verbs more than once.

can	could	may	might	must	should	would

1. Christian _____would_____ like to speak Romanian more.

2. He _____ speak Romanian every day.

3. Then he _____ practice his native language.

4. Someday Christian _____ visit Romania.

5. Then he _____ know the language better.

6. Jenny _____ add more stamps to her collection.

7. She _____ treat the stamps with care.

8. In the future, Jenny _____ give her stamp collection to her children.

Helping Verbs, continued

B. Add a helping verb to each sentence. Circle the main verb.

9. I _____ must _____ (study) for the math test tonight.

10. First I _____ review my notes.

11. Then I _____ read the chapters again.

12. I _____ ask my dad for some help.

13. He _____ certainly help me.

14. I know I _____ get an "A" on the test!

C. Write four sentences of your own. Use a helping verb from the box on page 51 in each sentence.

15. I _____

_____ .

16. I _____

_____ .

17. I _____

_____ .

18. I _____

_____ .

D. 19.–24. Edit the journal entry below. Add a helping verb to each sentence.

Journal Entry

June 1

I talk to the new girl in my class soon. I like to know her better. I be a big help to

her, too. I teach her to speak English. Maybe she tell me about her life in Bosnia.

Tomorrow I invite her to my house.

Revising and Editing Marks

∧   Add.

   Move to here.

   Replace with this.

   Take out.

∧   Add a comma.

⊙   Add a period.

≡   Capitalize.

╱   Make lower case.

Skills Review

A. Choose the form of the verb that best completes each sentence.

1. Patricia Polacco _____lived_____ on a farm in Michigan from 1944 until 1949.
   live / lived

2. In 1949, she _____ to Florida with her mother and her brother.
   move / moved

3. Patricia _____ many interesting people in Florida.
   meets / met

4. She _____ a learning disability when she was young.
   has / had

5. She _____ very well when she was a child.
   draw / drew

6. She _____ many different kinds of people growing up.
   meet / met

7. She _____ lucky today to remember them.
   feels / felt

8. She _____ her first children's book at age forty-one.
   writes / wrote

9. Now Patricia also _____ the pictures for her books.
   draws /drew

10. Today she _____ a Web site full of exciting information.
    has / had

B. Write the correct past tense form of the verb in parentheses.

11. Patricia _____studied_____ art in college. (**study**)

12. After college she _____ her husband. (**marry**)

13. Then Patricia _____ two children, a boy and a girl. (**have**)

14. Patricia's grandparents _____ storytellers. (**are**)

15. She _____ their stories to her own children. (**tell**)

16. Then Patricia _____ to write down her stories. (**begin**)

17. Her grandparents' stories _____ her books. (**inspire**)

18. In 1988, Patricia _____ an award for her book *The Keeping Quilt*. (**win**)

Skills Review, continued

C. Rewrite each sentence. Use the future tense.

19. I go on a long trip around the United States. _I will go / am going to go on a long trip around the United States._

20. I meet many interesting people. _____

_____

21. I ask questions about their lives and cultures. _____

_____

22. People tell me wonderful stories. _____

_____

23. I write a book about my trip. _____

_____

D. Circle the verb in each sentence. Underline the object if there is one. Tell if the verb is transitive or intransitive.

24. My neighbors (moved) here last month. _____intransitive_____

25. They speak mostly Japanese. _____

26. One day I took some cookies to them. _____

27. A girl my age answered the door. _____

28. She smiled happily. _____

29. Now Yuki and I play every day. _____

E. Write a helping verb to complete each of the sentences.

Helping Verbs	
could	might
would	can
should	must
may	

30. You ___should___ get to know many people.

31. Some people _____ tell interesting stories about their cultures.

32. You _____ be polite when you ask questions.

33. You _____ want to write down the answers.

34. You _____ learn more about yourself from listening to others.

35. Others _____ ask questions about you, too.

36. Then everyone _____ understand each other better.

Pronouns

A **pronoun** is a word that takes the place of a noun.

- A **subject pronoun** replaces the subject in a sentence.

  Example: **Lara** likes music.

       ↓

  She likes music.
  subject
  pronoun

Subject Pronouns						
I	you	he	she	it	we	they

- A **possessive pronoun** shows who owns something.

  Example: **Lara's** friend likes music, too.

       ↓

  Her friend likes music, too.
  possessive
  pronoun

Possessive Pronouns						
my	your	his	her	its	our	their

- An **antecedent** is the noun that the pronoun replaces.

  Example: **Lara** listens to music with **Lara's** friend.

     ↓   ↓
  antecedent   antecedent
     ↓   ↓

  She listens to music with **her** friend.
  subject   possessive
  pronoun   pronoun

A. Circle the antecedent in the first sentence in each pair. Then write the subject pronoun that replaces it to complete the second sentence.

1. (Ralph) is in a band. _____He_____ plays the drums.
   I / He

2. Ana is in the band, too. _____ plays the guitar.
   She / You

3. Luis does not play an instrument. _____ sings.
   We / He

4. The children like to play music together. _____ have fun.
   They / You

5. The music is fun to listen to. _____ is loud sometimes, though.
   It / We

6. Ralph, Ana, and Luis like loud music. _____ like each other, too.
   I / They

Pronouns, continued

B. Rewrite each sentence. Replace the underlined antecedent with a possessive pronoun.

7. Pedro and <u>Pedro's</u> friend like to do things together.

   Pedro and his friend like to do things together.

   _____

8. Gina likes to take <u>Gina's</u> dog for a walk.

   _____

   _____

9. <u>The dog's</u> name is Pepper. _____

   _____

10. Sometimes Pedro, Gina, and Pepper go to the park on <u>Pedro, Gina, and Pepper's</u> walk. _____

   _____

11. Gina says, "We can play ball with <u>Gina's</u> dog." _____

   _____

12. Then they find a tree and sit in <u>the tree's</u> shade. _____

   _____

13. Pedro says, "Gina, I am glad that you are <u>Pedro's</u> friend." _____

   _____

C. Add pronouns to complete the sentences.

Beth is new at school. ____She____ does not have any friends and feels lonely. One day
                        14.

Beth hears some music. _____ is coming from Mr. Wang's room. Beth peeks into
                        15.

_____ room. A boy sees Beth and says, "_____ name is Juan. Would
16.   **17.**

_____ like to sing with us?" Beth is not lonely anymore. _____ has made
18.   **19.**

a connection by singing with _____ new friends.
                             20.

D. 21.–23. Tell your partner about something that you like to do with your friends. Use three pronouns.

Example: "I like to go bike riding with my friends. We ride our bikes on the bike path by the river."

Pronoun Agreement

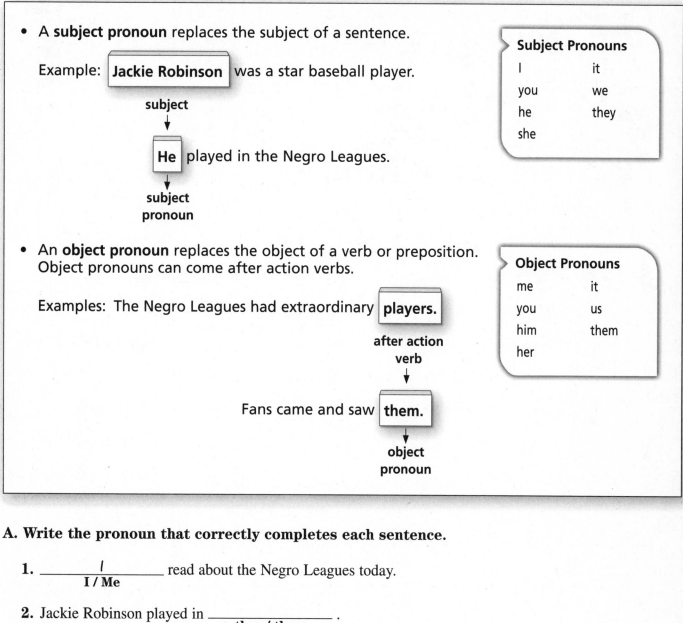

- A **subject pronoun** replaces the subject of a sentence.

  Example: | Jackie Robinson | was a star baseball player.

  subject

  | He | played in the Negro Leagues.

  subject
  pronoun

  Subject Pronouns

I	it
you	we
he	they
she	

- An **object pronoun** replaces the object of a verb or preposition. Object pronouns can come after action verbs.

  Examples: The Negro Leagues had extraordinary | players.

  after action
  verb

  Fans came and saw | them.

  object
  pronoun

  Object Pronouns

me	it
you	us
him	them
her	

A. Write the pronoun that correctly completes each sentence.

1. _____ _I_ _____ read about the Negro Leagues today.
   I / Me

2. Jackie Robinson played in _____ .
   they / them

3. _____ was a real star.
   He / Him

4. Branch Rickey heard good things about _____ .
   he / him

5. Branch Rickey wanted _____ to play in the Major Leagues.
   he / him

6. Black baseball players were not allowed to play in _____ .
   they / them

7. That does not sound fair to _____ .
   I / me

Pronoun Agreement, continued

B. Add pronouns to complete the sentences.

A Baseball Fan!

Julia is a baseball fan. _____She_____ loves baseball. Dad gives _____
                                 8.   9.

a book about baseball. _____ tells all about the history of the game. The book tells
                                   10.

about a lot of famous players. Jackie Robinson is one of _____ . Julia reads all about
                                                       11.

_____ . Jackie Robinson was a star player in the Negro League. _____
         12.   13.

joined the Brooklyn Dodgers in 1947. _____ were looking for the best players for
                                   14.

_____ team. _____ thought Jackie Robinson might be just the man.
     15.   16.

Julia's Dad has another surprise for _____ . "Do you want to go to the baseball
                                       17.

game with _____ ?" Dad asks. Julia and Dad go to the game. _____
         18.   19.

watch the teammates play and have fun. Julia and Dad cheer for _____ .
                                                                 20.

C. 21.–29. Edit the report below. Use subject and object pronouns correctly.

Revising and Editing Marks

∧	Add.
↶	Move to here.
↶	Replace with this.
ϱ	Take out.
∧	Add a comma.
⊙	Add a period.
≡	Capitalize.
/	Make lower case.

Grandma remembers the Negro Leagues. She tells I about they. Her went to some of the games. The players were heroes to she. Them did not make a lot of money, though. Life on the road was hard for them. Grandma had a favorite player. Him was Jackie Robinson. Her remembers the spring of 1947. Branch Rickey wanted he to play for the Brooklyn Dodgers. Grandma liked Mr. Rickey. He was a hero to she, too.

Subject, Possessive, and Reflexive Pronouns

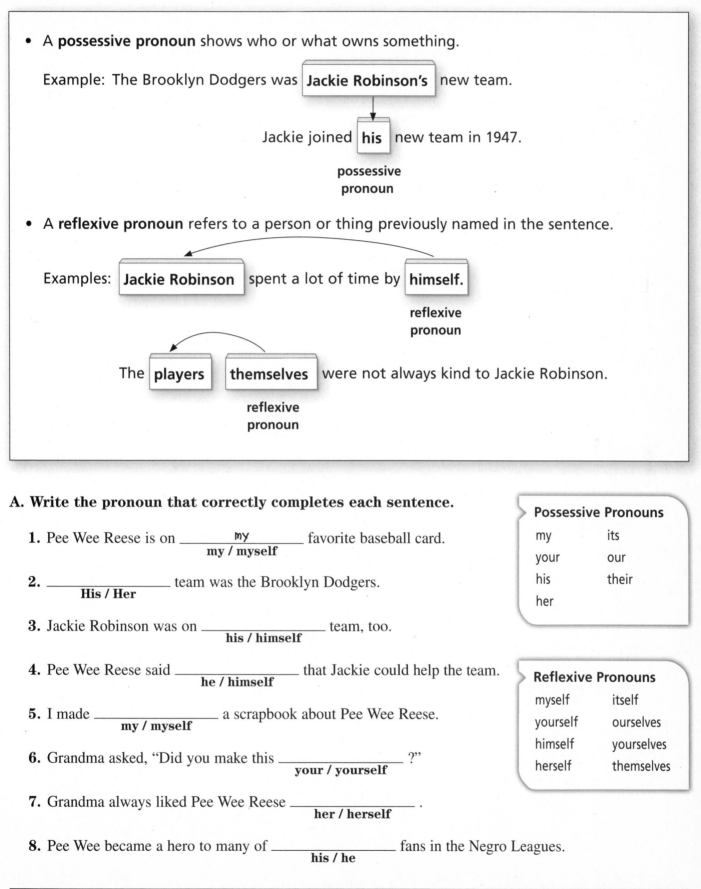

- A **possessive pronoun** shows who or what owns something.

  Example: The Brooklyn Dodgers was | Jackie Robinson's | new team.

  Jackie joined | his | new team in 1947.

  possessive pronoun

- A **reflexive pronoun** refers to a person or thing previously named in the sentence.

  Examples: | Jackie Robinson | spent a lot of time by | himself. |

  reflexive pronoun

  The | players | themselves | were not always kind to Jackie Robinson.

  reflexive pronoun

A. Write the pronoun that correctly completes each sentence.

1. Pee Wee Reese is on _____my_____ favorite baseball card.
   my / myself

2. _____ team was the Brooklyn Dodgers.
   His / Her

3. Jackie Robinson was on _____ team, too.
   his / himself

4. Pee Wee Reese said _____ that Jackie could help the team.
   he / himself

5. I made _____ a scrapbook about Pee Wee Reese.
   my / myself

6. Grandma asked, "Did you make this _____ ?"
   your / yourself

7. Grandma always liked Pee Wee Reese _____ .
   her / herself

8. Pee Wee became a hero to many of _____ fans in the Negro Leagues.
   his / he

Possessive Pronouns	
my	its
your	our
his	their
her	

Reflexive Pronouns	
myself	itself
yourself	ourselves
himself	yourselves
herself	themselves

Subject, Possessive, and Reflexive Pronouns, continued

B. Add pronouns to complete the sentences.

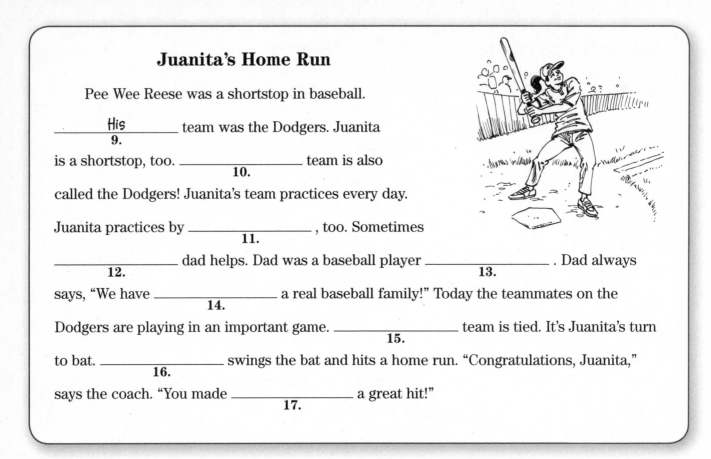

Juanita's Home Run

Pee Wee Reese was a shortstop in baseball.

_____His_____ team was the Dodgers. Juanita
9.

is a shortstop, too. _____ team is also
10.

called the Dodgers! Juanita's team practices every day.

Juanita practices by _____ , too. Sometimes
11.

_____ dad helps. Dad was a baseball player _____ . Dad always
12.   13.

says, "We have _____ a real baseball family!" Today the teammates on the
14.

Dodgers are playing in an important game. _____ team is tied. It's Juanita's turn
15.

to bat. _____ swings the bat and hits a home run. "Congratulations, Juanita,"
16.

says the coach. "You made _____ a great hit!"
17.

C. 18.–26. Edit the letter below. Use pronouns correctly.

Dear Aunt Jean,

    Yesterday myself went to the Baseball Hall of Fame. I saw a picture of Pee Wee

Reese. Jackie Robinson was himself teammate. Themselves team was the Brooklyn

Dodgers. Pee Wee was a shortstop. Jackie had played shortstop his. Pee Wee's

teammates did not want Jackie on the team. Themselves started a petition. Pee

Wee refused to sign they petition. He his thought good players should be able to play

on he team. That's what I think my!

Love,

Tony

© Hampton-Brown

Pronouns

A **pronoun** takes the place of a noun. The noun that the pronoun replaces is the **antecedent**.

- A **pronoun** must agree in type with its antecedent. Use *she* and *her* to tell about females. Use *he, him,* and *his* to tell about males.

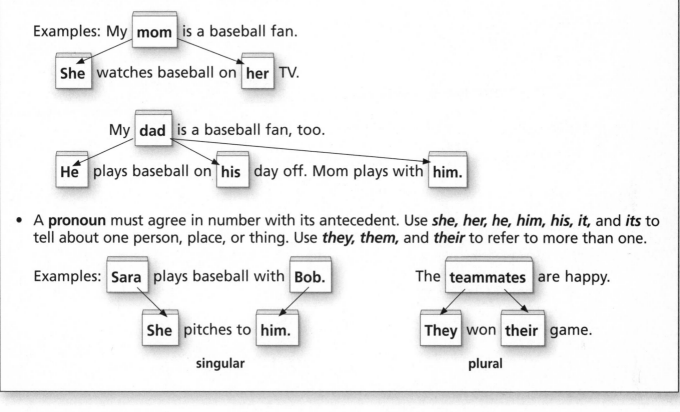

- A **pronoun** must agree in number with its antecedent. Use *she, her, he, him, his, it,* and *its* to tell about one person, place, or thing. Use *they, them,* and *their* to refer to more than one.

A. Write the pronoun that correctly completes the second sentence in each pair.

1. Cincinnati is a city in Ohio. _____*It*_____ is near Louisville.
   It / They

2. The Dodgers went to Cincinnati. _____ played in a small ballpark there.
   It / They

3. Jackie Robinson was on the field. Some Cincinnati fans were mean to _____ .
   her / him

4. Pee Wee Reese wanted to do what was right. _____ walked over to Jackie Robinson.
   He / They

5. Pee Wee smiled at Jackie. Then Pee Wee put an arm around _____ shoulders.
   her / his

6. My grandma was at that game. _____ watched from the stands.
   She / They

7. Grandma said that there was silence. It was a special moment for _____ .
   her / them

© Hampton-Brown

Pronouns, continued

B. Add pronouns to complete the sentences.

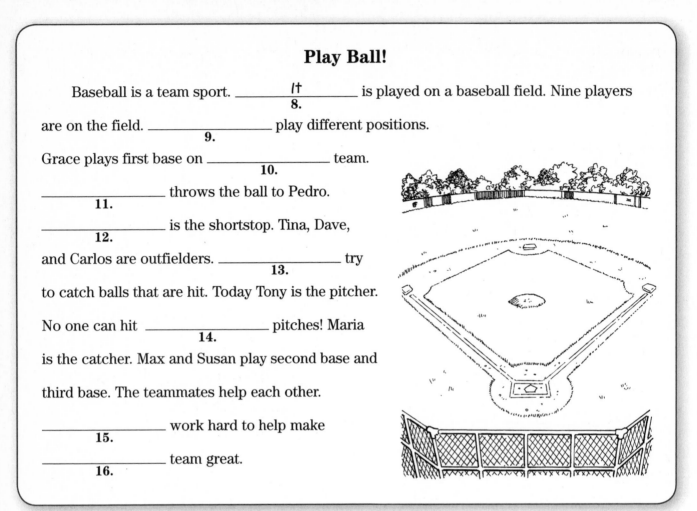

Play Ball!

Baseball is a team sport. _____*It*_____ is played on a baseball field. Nine players
8.

are on the field. _____ play different positions.
9.

Grace plays first base on _____ team.
10.

_____ throws the ball to Pedro.
11.

_____ is the shortstop. Tina, Dave,
12.

and Carlos are outfielders. _____ try
13.

to catch balls that are hit. Today Tony is the pitcher.

No one can hit _____ pitches! Maria
14.

is the catcher. Max and Susan play second base and

third base. The teammates help each other.

_____ work hard to help make
15.

_____ team great.
16.

**C. 17.–23. Edit the sports story below. Fix the pronouns so that they
agree with their antecedents.**

Dodgers Win

Today the Dodgers played a great game. It won by one run. Sara was the

pitcher. He allowed only two hits. One of it was a single. The other was a double.

Sara also scored the winning run. The pitcher pitched the ball to them. Sara hit

a home run! The teammates all hit well. She all played well in the field, too. The

parents were proud of its children. The children were proud of his team.

Revising and Editing Marks	
∧	Add.
↶	Move to here.
⋀	Replace with this.
ˢ	Take out.
∧	Add a comma.
⊙	Add a period.
≡	Capitalize.
/	Make lower case.

Possessive Nouns and Pronouns

A **possessive noun** shows who or what owns or has something. Possessive nouns have
an **apostrophe** (**'**).

- Use **'s** to show that one person or thing owns something. Use **s'** to show that two or more
  people or things own or have something.

  Examples: *Neighbors of Amir* start a community garden.

  | Amir**'**s neighbors | start a community garden.

  The *garden of the neighbors* is green.

  | The neighbors**'** garden | is green.

A **possessive pronoun** shows who or what owns or has something.

- Use these pronouns before a noun: *my, your, his, her, its, our, their.*

  Examples: | His | neighbors start a garden. | Their | garden is green.

  possessive   noun   possessive   noun
  pronoun   pronoun

- Use these pronouns without a noun: *mine, yours, his, hers, its, ours, theirs.*

  Examples: The neighbors are | his.   The green garden is | theirs.

  possessive   possessive
  pronoun   pronoun

**A. Complete the sentences. Use possessive nouns to write the words
in parentheses.**

1. _____ India's cities _____ are really big. (**cities of India**)

2. Amir is from India, but he lives in one of _____ . (**cities of America**)

3. _____ plant a garden. (**neighbors of Amir**)

4. It reminds Amir of his _____ . (**rug of parents**)

5. The _____ are growing. (**leaves of vegetables**)

6. That makes the _____ a soothing green. (**color of garden**)

© Hampton-Brown

Possessive Nouns and Pronouns, continued

B. Add a possessive pronoun from the boxes to complete the sentences.

7. My neighbors and I have a community garden. The garden is _____ours_____ .

8. I grow eggplants. The eggplants are _____ .

9. The eggplants have a strange color. _____ color is a pale purple.

10. José grows carrots. _____ carrots grow under the ground.

11. Cara is growing vegetables, too. The onion plants are _____ .

12. The Browns grow cauliflower. These plants are _____ .

13. The garden belongs to all of us. We water _____ garden every day.

14. I am watering the garden today. It is _____ turn to water.

15. Cara is weeding. It is _____ turn to weed.

> **Possessive Pronouns Before Nouns**
>
> | | |
> |---|---|
> | my | our |
> | your | their |
> | his, her, its | |

> **Possessive Pronouns with No Noun**
>
> | | |
> |---|---|
> | mine | ours |
> | yours | theirs |
> | his, hers, its | |

C. 16.–24. Imagine that Amir wrote the following letter about the community garden. Edit the letter. Use possessive nouns and pronouns correctly.

> **Revising and Editing Marks**
>
> | | |
> |---|---|
> | ∧ | Add. |
> | ⟲ | Move to here. |
> | ⋀ | Replace with this. |
> | ⌐ | Take out. |
> | ∧, | Add a comma. |
> | ⊙ | Add a period. |
> | ≡ | Capitalize. |
> | / | Make lower case. |

Dear Mom and Dad,

I finally met some of mine neighbors. They started a community garden. Theirs garden is right in the middle of the neighborhood. The gardens plants are green and beautiful. The garden reminded me of yours Persian rug! I put in some plants, too. The eggplants and cauliflower are my, but the garden belongs to all of us. It is our. We all take care of ours garden! How is your garden? I hope ours garden will be as nice as your!

Love,

Amir

Negative Sentences

- Use a **negative word** to make a negative sentence.

  > **Negative Words**
  >
  > | no | none | not | never | neither | hardly |
  > |----|------|-----|-------|---------|--------|
  > | isn't | aren't | weren't | nobody | nothing | nowhere |
  > | hasn't | shouldn't | couldn't | didn't | can't | won't |

  Examples: Amir **never** knew his neighbors before the community garden.

  Amir **didn't** know his neighbors before the community garden.

  Amir knew **none** of his neighbors before the community garden.

- Use only **one** negative word in a sentence.

  Examples: **Incorrect:** There **aren't no** tires in the garden.

  Correct: There are **no** tires in the garden.   There **aren't** any tires in the garden.

A. Make the sentences negative. Use the words in parentheses.

1. My neighbors have a garden. (**never**) _____

_____

2. I grow corn in my garden. (**won't**) _____

_____

3. Sunish knows about gardens. (**nothing**) _____

_____

4. Weeds are in this garden. (**nowhere**) _____

_____

5. There are rabbits in my garden. (**no**) _____

_____

Negative Sentences, continued

B. Rewrite each sentence correctly. Make sure you keep it a negative sentence.

6. Jake hasn't never lived in Cleveland. <u>Jake has never</u>
   <u>lived in Cleveland.</u>

7. Not nobody pulled the weeds from this garden. _____

   _____

   _____

8. Hardly none of my tomatoes grew this year. _____

   _____

9. Nothing won't grow unless you water the garden. _____

   _____

10. Tina didn't plant no carrots this year. _____

    _____

11. No neighbors never put trash in my garden. _____

    _____

12. There isn't nobody who grows cauliflower except me! _____

    _____

C. 13.–20. Edit the story about the Little Red Hen. Use negative words correctly.

Revising and Editing Marks

∧	Add.
⤳	Move to here.
⌁	Replace with this.
ዒ	Take out.
∧	Add a comma.
⨀	Add a period.
≡	Capitalize.
/	Make lower case.

The Little Red Hen

Haven't you never heard the story of the Little Red Hen? Not nobody helped her grow the wheat. Nobody didn't help her cut the wheat. Not none of her friends helped her make the wheat into flour. "Who will help me bake bread?" she asked. Nobody said nothing. The Little Red Hen baked her bread. All of her friends wanted some. She didn't give none to nobody. "You didn't never help," she said. "I'll eat the bread myself!"

66

Indefinite Pronouns

Use an **indefinite pronoun** when you do not know the name of a specific person, place, or thing.

- Most indefinite pronouns are **singular**. Use them with **singular verbs**.

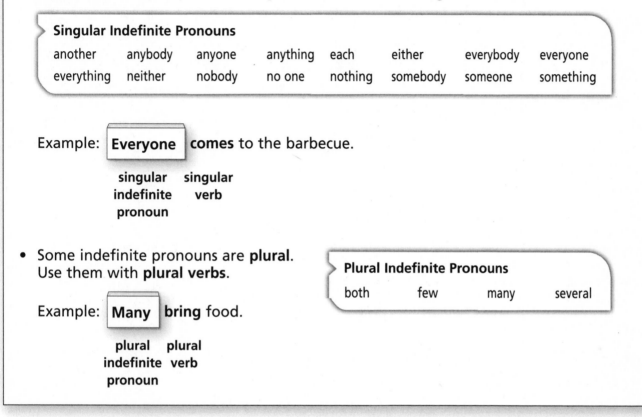

Singular Indefinite Pronouns

| another | anybody | anyone | anything | each | either | everybody | everyone |
| everything | neither | nobody | no one | nothing | somebody | someone | something |

Example: **Everyone** **comes** to the barbecue.

singular   singular
indefinite   verb
pronoun

- Some indefinite pronouns are **plural**. Use them with **plural verbs**.

Plural Indefinite Pronouns

| both | few | many | several |

Example: **Many** **bring** food.

plural   plural
indefinite   verb
pronoun

A. Circle the indefinite pronoun in each sentence. Then write the verb that correctly completes the sentence.

1. (Someone) _____builds_____ a barbecue in the neighborhood.
   build / builds

2. Several of the neighbors _____ with vegetables that they grow.
   arrive / arrives

3. No one _____ the party.
   plan / plans

4. Everyone _____ it.
   enjoy / enjoys

5. Many _____ off their vegetables.
   show / shows

6. A few of them _____ harvests.
   trade / trades

7. Everybody _____ the food.
   eat / eats

© Hampton-Brown

Indefinite Pronouns, continued

B. Add indefinite pronouns to complete the sentences.

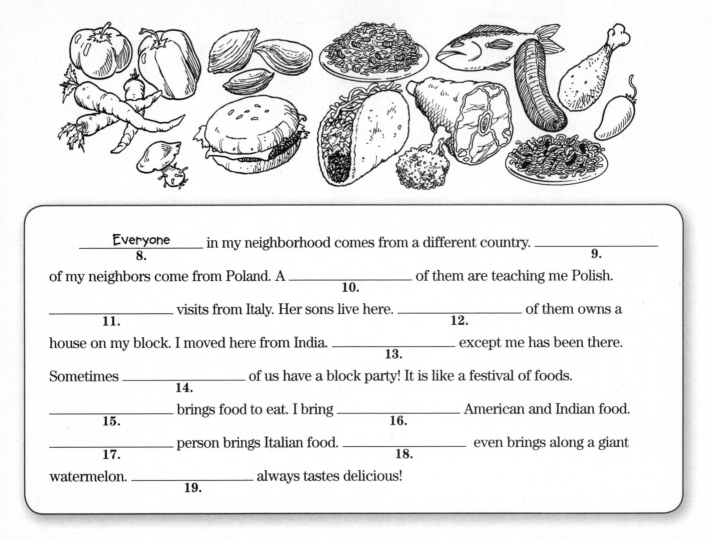

_____Everyone_____ in my neighborhood comes from a different country. _____
     8.   **9.**

of my neighbors come from Poland. A _____ of them are teaching me Polish.
                                              10.

_____ visits from Italy. Her sons live here. _____ of them owns a
     11.   **12.**

house on my block. I moved here from India. _____ except me has been there.
                                                        13.

Sometimes _____ of us have a block party! It is like a festival of foods.
              14.

_____ brings food to eat. I bring _____ American and Indian food.
     15.   **16.**

_____ person brings Italian food. _____ even brings along a giant
     17.   **18.**

watermelon. _____ always tastes delicious!
                 19.

C. 20.–27. Edit the letter. Use the indefinite pronouns and the verbs correctly.

Revising and Editing Marks	
∧	Add.
↶	Move to here.
∧	Replace with this.
⌀	Take out.
∧	Add a comma.
⊙	Add a period.
≡	Capitalize.
/	Make lower case.

Dear Grandpa,

My neighbors have a community garden. Everyone grow something good to

eat. Several plants carrots. Many of us grows corn. A few of my neighbors likes

watermelon. That's why we have watermelon plants! Right now everything look ripe.

Everybody pick the ripe food. Many of us trades our harvests. Somebody say,

"Let's have a party! We can eat the food we grew in our garden!"

Love,

Alyssa

Progressive Forms of Verbs

The **present progressive** form of a verb tells about an action that is happening now.

- The present progressive uses the helping verb *am, is,* or *are* with the **present participle** or the **–ing form** of the verb.

Examples: I | am | | starting | a community garden.

am ✚ starting ═ present progressive

Mom | is | | helping | me.

is ✚ helping ═ present progressive

We | are | | working | hard.

are ✚ working ═ present progressive

The **past progressive** form of a verb tells about an action that happened over time in the past.

- The past progressive uses the helping verb *was* or *were* with the **present participle**.

Examples: Yesterday I | was | | planting | seeds.

was ✚ planting ═ past progressive

Mom and I | were | | watering | them.

were ✚ watering ═ past progressive

A. Complete the paragraphs. Use the present progressive form of the verb in the first paragraph. Use the past progressive form in the second.

People _____are enjoying_____ community gardens all around America. They
   1. enjoy

_____ empty lots into gardens. I _____ to start a garden
   2. turn   **3. try**

in my community. My best friend _____ to help me.
                                4. go

Last week we _____ our teacher about our community garden.
                5. tell

I _____ what we had to do. First Mrs. Chan _____ carefully.
   6. explain   **7. listen**

Then she _____ if she could help!
         8. ask

Progressive Forms of Verbs, continued

B. Rewrite each sentence with the present progressive form of the verb. Then rewrite it with the past progressive form.

I look for a spot for a garden.

9. _I am looking for a spot for a garden._ _____

_____

10. _____

_____

My mom wonders about an empty lot down the street.

11. _____

_____

12. _____

_____

We call the owner of the lot.

13. _____

_____

14. _____

_____

C. 15.–26. Imagine that you are telling a friend about what you are growing in your garden. Edit the paragraphs. Use the present and past progressive forms of the verbs.

Revising and Editing Marks

∧	Add.
⟳	Move to here.
∧	Replace with this.
℘	Take out.
∧̦	Add a comma.
⊙	Add a period.
≡	Capitalize.
/	Make lower case.

Every year I am grow something different in my garden. Last year I were grow watermelons. They was growing on a vine. The watermelons getting very big. One day I was harvest them. Then I eating them. Yum! My family and I enjoying them!

This year I growing tomatoes. I is watch them grow. Every day they are get riper. I is look forward to my ripe tomatoes. They are make me hungry!

© Hampton-Brown

Skills Review

A. Read the sentences. Circle the correct pronoun.

1. _____(I)/ Me_____ grew up in the state of Kentucky.

2. _____It / They_____ is where Pee Wee Reese grew up.

3. _____We / Us_____ both grew up in the city of Ekron.

4. Pee Wee Reese was famous. Have you heard of _____he / him_____ ?

5. _____He / They_____ was a baseball player on the Brooklyn Dodgers.

6. Jackie Robinson was a player for _____they / them_____ , too.

7. My grandma was a Brooklyn Dodgers fan. _____She / Them_____ went to see Jackie Robinson play.

8. Jackie grew up near _____she / her_____ in Cairo, Georgia.

B. Write the pronouns that correctly complete the sentences.

9. I like to garden by _____myself_____ .
   mine / myself

10. This flower garden is _____ .
    my / mine

11. The flowers almost seem to take care of _____ .
    theirs / themselves

12. I water the neighbors' garden, too. _____ flowers are very pretty.
    Their / Theirs

13. I like to play baseball with _____ neighborhood friends.
    my / myself

14. We have _____ own team.
    our / ours

15. We formed it all by _____ .
    ours / ourselves

16. Sometimes we play other neighborhood teams at _____ field.
    our / ourselves

17. Other times we play at _____ .
    their / theirs

Skills Review, continued

C. Rewrite each sentence correctly. Make sure you keep it a negative sentence.

18. Marco hasn't never planted a garden. _Marco hasn't ever planted a garden._ _____

_____

19. He doesn't buy vegetables at the store, neither. _____

_____

20. Marco hardly eats no vegetables. _____

_____

21. Nobody never told him how good vegetables are. _____

_____

22. He hasn't got nothing to lose by trying some. _____

_____

D. Complete each sentence with an indefinite pronoun from the box. Use pronouns that agree with the verbs.

Indefinite Pronouns
nobody
few
each
many
everyone
anything
nothing
several

23. In my family, _____everyone_____ likes tomatoes.

24. _____ of us eat them straight from our garden.

25. A _____ of us make them into a sauce.

26. _____ is as good as homemade tomato sauce!

27. _____ of us shares tomatoes with our friends.

28. _____ is a good excuse for a neighborhood party.

29. _____ of our neighbors come.

30. _____ wants to miss a good party!

E. Write the progressive form of the verb to correctly complete each sentence.

31. Right now Joshua _____is playing_____ baseball. (**play**)

32. I _____ him. (**watch**)

33. Last winter he _____ basketballs with the team. (**shoot**)

34. Before that he _____ soccer balls. (**kick**)

35. During soccer the kids _____ a lot! (**run**)

Skills Review and Practice Tests

A. Write the verb that correctly completes each sentence.

1. In the past, people _____ *came* _____ to the United States from all over the world.
   will come / came

2. These days they still _____ here.
   move / moved

3. My great-grandmother _____ up in Russia a long time ago.
   grows / grew

4. Now she _____ in New York City.
   lives / lived

5. When Great-Grandma first _____ , she had a hard time fitting in.
   arrived / arrives

6. Now she _____ in fine.
   will fit / fits

7. Soon Great-Grandma _____ Russia again.
   will visit / visited

8. She _____ her old friends and family.
   saw / is going to see

9. Right now she _____ her new friends.
   enjoys / enjoyed

10. Right now Great-Grandma _____ happy to belong to both cultures!
    was / is

B. Complete the sentences. Write the past tense of the verbs in parentheses. Use pages 450–451 of the Handbook to help you.

11. Great-Grandma _____*arrived*_____ in this country a long time ago. (**arrive**)

12. Great-Grandma _____ me about her trip. (**tell**)

13. She _____ into New York City. (**sail**)

14. She _____ very excited to arrive. (**is**)

15. Great-Grandma _____ her hands and jumped up and down. (**clap**)

16. When Great-Grandma walked off the boat, she _____ only one bag. (**carry**)

17. The bag _____ everything she owned inside. (**have**)

18. Great-Grandma _____ hard to fit in. (**try**)

19. She _____ herself English. (**teach**)

20. She _____ to feel at home in her new country. (**begin**)

C. Read the passage. Read each item carefully. Choose the best answer. Mark your answer.

Today more than 8,000,000 people lived [1] in New York City. In the future, the city grows [2] even bigger! People move to New York City from all over the world. There are many different cultures in New York City. People learn new ways of living. They hold onto their old cultures and beliefs, too. People fit into both their new groups and their old groups.

Right now New York will have [3] a part called Chinatown. Today this was [4] the largest Chinatown in the United States. Many Chinese Americans live and work in Chinatown. Tourists visit, too. They learn about the Chinese American culture. They visit Chinese restaurants and shops.

A long time ago, when Great-Grandma moved to New York City, it was not as big as it is now. It was the same in some ways, though. People from different cultures lived and tried [5] to fit in together. Today in my New York City neighborhood, people from many different cultures live together. We are different in some ways, but we are the same in some ways, too. When we play sports, we all fit in together. We do not look at our differences. We just help each other won [6] the game.

21. In number 1, lived is best written —
Ⓐ will live
Ⓑ live
Ⓒ livd
Ⓓ as it is written

22. In number 2, grows is best written —
Ⓕ grew
Ⓖ growed
Ⓗ will grow
Ⓙ as it is written

23. In number 3, will have is best written —
Ⓐ haved
Ⓑ had
Ⓒ has
Ⓓ as it is written

24. In number 4, was is best written —
Ⓕ is
Ⓖ are
Ⓗ will be
Ⓙ as it is written

25. In number 5, tried is best written —
Ⓐ will try
Ⓑ tryed
Ⓒ try
Ⓓ as it is written

26. In number 6, won is best written —
Ⓕ will win
Ⓖ winned
Ⓗ win
Ⓙ as it is written

Skills Review and Practice Tests, continued

D. Write the pronouns that complete the sentences correctly.

myself	they	them	him	it	theirs
my	himself	his	mine	me	I

How do people create connections? _____ discover common interests.
                                              27.

Many people share a common interest in sports. Sports can bridge a gap between

_____ . That's because sports is a common interest of _____ .
        28.   **29.**

Some people play baseball. _____ is a sport that brings people together from all
                                    30.

around the world.

Baseball helped _____ dad bridge a gap. Dad played baseball in college.
                        31.

That helped _____ make connections. Dad met some of _____
                    32.   **33.**

best friends playing baseball. Dad taught _____ to play baseball. Now Dad is
                                                    34.

teaching _____ . This baseball glove is _____ . I bought it
                35.   **36.**

_____ ! Maybe _____ can use baseball to bridge the gap with
        37.   **38.**

people, too!

E. Write the indefinite pronoun that correctly completes each sentence.

39. In my city, _____nothing_____ brings the kids together like sports!
                      both / nothing

40. _____ seems to love baseball.
      Everybody / Many

41. _____ of the kids play on city baseball teams.
      Several / No one

42. _____ shares a common interest in baseball.
      Everyone / Many

43. _____ of my best friends come from the same part of the city.
      Anyone / Both

44. _____ of us knows how lucky we are that baseball bridged a gap!
      Few / Each

© Hampton-Brown

F. Read the passage. Read each item carefully. Choose the best answer. Mark your answer.

Isabelle is doing a research report on the history of baseball for a school assignment. Her chose hers topic because she loves baseball. Isabelle is reading about the All-American Girls
<u>   </u>
                        1
Baseball League. That topic is very interesting to <u>him</u>. That is because Isabelle's mom and grandma
                                                        2
played baseball instead of softball. Isabelle <u>hers</u> plays baseball. <u>Each</u> of her friends do, too. This is
                                                3   **4**
what Isabelle writes about the league:

The All-American Girls Baseball League started in 1943. During World War II, many Major League baseball players went to war. There were not a lot of players left to play baseball. Phillip Wrigley was the owner of the Chicago Cubs. Wrigley decided to start a women's baseball league to play in the Major League parks. Women from all over the United States and Canada came to try out for the teams. Baseball bridged a gap for all the women. <u>Its was a common interest of hers</u>.
                                                                                    5
The All-American Girls Baseball League was a great success. Thousands of fans came to watch the games. At first there were only four teams. By 1948, there were ten of <u>they</u>. The All-American Girls
                                                                                    6
Baseball League ended in 1954.

45. In number 1, the correct way to write the sentence is —
Ⓐ She chose hers topic because she loves baseball.
Ⓑ She chose her topic because she loves baseball.
Ⓒ Her chose hers topic because her loves baseball.
Ⓓ Her chose her topic because she loves baseball.

46. In number 2, <u>him</u> is best written —
Ⓕ they
Ⓖ his
Ⓗ her
Ⓙ as it is written

47. In number 3, <u>hers</u> is best written —
Ⓐ them
Ⓑ himself
Ⓒ herself
Ⓓ as it is written

48. In number 4, <u>Each</u> is best written —
Ⓕ Nobody
Ⓖ Everyone
Ⓗ Many
Ⓙ as it is written

49. In number 5, the correct way to write the sentence is —
Ⓐ It was a common interest of hers.
Ⓑ Its was a common interest of them.
Ⓒ Its was a common interest of hers.
Ⓓ It was a common interest of theirs.

50. In number 6, <u>they</u> is best written —
Ⓕ them
Ⓖ theirs
Ⓗ themselves
Ⓙ as it is written

Adjectives, Adverbs, and Prepositional Phrases

Adjectives, adverbs, and **prepositional phrases** add details to sentences.

- An **adjective** describes a noun or pronoun. Adjectives can tell:

which one	I liked the (first) folk tale I read.
how many	There are (three) folk tales in the book.
what something or someone is like	This is an (interesting) story.

- An **adverb** often tells more about a verb. Adverbs can tell:

how	The folk tale ended (happily).
where	Folk tales are read (everywhere).
when	This book is going on sale (soon).

- A **prepositional phrase** starts with a **preposition** and ends with a noun or pronoun. Prepositional phrases can tell:

where	This folk tale is (from Vietnam).
when	We listened to the tale (in the afternoon).

A. Choose an adjective, adverb, or prepositional phrase from the box to complete each sentence.

for two days	many	usually	after	during the year	exciting	at the park	wide

1. _____ Many _____ families have traditions that are important to them.

2. Family members _____ share these traditions.

3. Every year Mika's family has an _____ party.

4. They celebrate all the hard work the family has done _____ .

5. This year the celebration lasted _____ .

6. Next year the family will celebrate _____ .

7. The park is located beside a _____ lake.

8. _____ lunch, everyone can rent boats and sail on the lake.

B. Complete the sentences with the type of word or phrase in parentheses. Choose from the words and phrases in the box.

> **Some Adjectives, Adverbs, and Prepositional Phrases**
>
> | | |
> |---|---|
> | with us | wonderful |
> | in our house | hard |
> | in the garden | often |
> | at the store | great |
> | long | important |
> | interesting | |

9. My grandmother came to live _____with us_____ last year. (**prepositional phrase**)

10. She had to take a _____ trip from Vietnam to America. (**adjective**)

11. Grandma brought a _____ tradition to America. (**adjective**)

12. Every spring Grandma plants vegetable seeds _____ . (**prepositional phrase**)

13. Now every spring I work _____ with Grandma. (**adverb**)

14. Grandma showed me a _____ tradition I can share with my children some day. (**adjective**)

15. Grandma shops for food from Vietnam _____ . (**prepositional phrase**)

16. She prepares special dinners for us _____ . (**adverb**)

C. Complete each sentence with an adjective, adverb, or prepositional phrase that makes sense.

"The Rooster and the Jewel" is a ____Vietnamese____ folk tale. In this _____ story,
    17.   18.

a _____ rooster searches _____ for something to eat. He looks in many
      19.   20.

places such as _____ and _____ . _____ he finds a jewel,
                21.   22.   23.

but it is worthless to him.

D. 24.–26. Tell a partner the story of a family tradition that you know about. Use adjectives, adverbs, and prepositional phrases to make your story more interesting.

Example: "Tron's family has an unusual tradition. Every year they plant a tree in a public park."

78

Adjectives

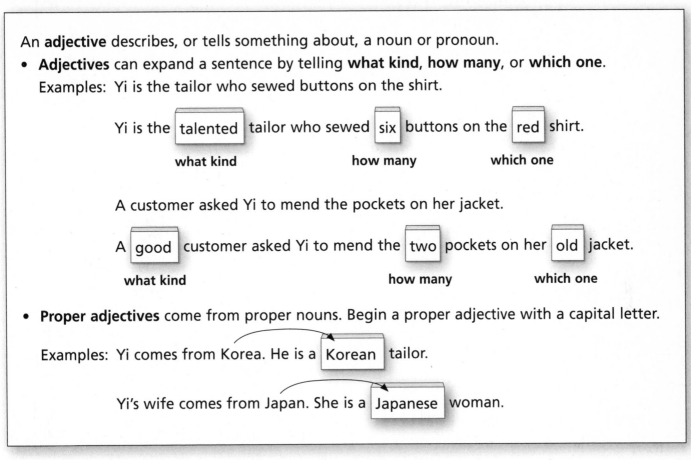

An **adjective** describes, or tells something about, a noun or pronoun.

- **Adjectives** can expand a sentence by telling **what kind**, **how many**, or **which one**.
  Examples: Yi is the tailor who sewed buttons on the shirt.

  Yi is the ⬚talented⬚ tailor who sewed ⬚six⬚ buttons on the ⬚red⬚ shirt.
          what kind   **how many**   **which one**

  A customer asked Yi to mend the pockets on her jacket.

  A ⬚good⬚ customer asked Yi to mend the ⬚two⬚ pockets on her ⬚old⬚ jacket.
    what kind   **how many**   **which one**

- **Proper adjectives** come from proper nouns. Begin a proper adjective with a capital letter.

  Examples: Yi comes from Korea. He is a ⬚Korean⬚ tailor.

  Yi's wife comes from Japan. She is a ⬚Japanese⬚ woman.

A. Complete each sentence with an adjective from the box. Use each adjective only once.

famous	Chinese	both	strong
Canadian	kind	wonderful	

1. Paul Yee is a _____famous_____ writer.

2. He is a _____ citizen who grew up in Vancouver.

3. Paul lost _____ parents when he was young.

4. A _____ aunt raised Paul and his brother.

5. Paul's aunt was a _____ woman.

6. She taught Paul and his brother the ways of the _____ people.

7. Paul's stories are a _____ mix of history and imagination.

Adjectives, continued

B. Expand each sentence by writing an adjective that makes sense in the blank. Choose adjectives from the box. Use at least one proper adjective.

Some Adjectives	
Chinese	poor
northern	small
American	wealthy
large	hairy
talented	good

8. San Francisco has a ____large____ Chinese community.

9. The first _____ immigrants came from China in 1850.

10. Some Chinese immigrants were _____ merchants.

11. Many _____ people came from China at that time, too.

12. They went to work in the gold mines

of _____ California.

13. They also opened _____ shops in San Francisco.

14. Yenna's father became a

_____ tailor.

15. Yenna and her mother were also

_____ tailors.

C. 16.–20. In the story "Ginger for the Heart," Yenna might have written the letter below. Circle five nouns in the letter. Then edit the letter by adding adjectives that tell about the nouns.

Revising and Editing Marks

∧	Add.
⟳	Move to here.
∧	Replace with this.
℘	Take out.
⌃	Add a comma.
⊙	Add a period.
≡	Capitalize.
/	Make lower case.

My Dear,

Each day I miss seeing your face. I think of your eyes. The winter here makes

life difficult. I still sew in the tower. I always have work to do. I sew for hours each

day. The daughter of a tailor has a hard life. I spend each night thinking of our

times together. I hope that soon we will spend days together again.

Yours,

Yenna

Compound Predicates

- A **verb** tells what the subject in a sentence is or does.

  Example: The **twins play** in the park.

      subject   verb

- A **compound predicate** has two or more verbs for the same subject. Compound predicates are joined by a **conjunction**, such as *and* or *or*.

  Example: The **twins play** in the park **and eat** lunch at the picnic table.

      subject   verb   conjunction   verb

- Both **verbs** in a compound predicate **agree with their subject**.

  Example: One **twin takes** piano lessons and **plays** baseball.

          singular   singular
          subject   verbs

A. Complete the compound predicate in each sentence. Use words from the box.

is still used in France	test newborn babies for deafness
is not the same everywhere	can take lessons
communicate their needs	hire teachers for them
can share their needs	can help language learning

1. Sign language exists in many countries and _____is not the same everywhere_____ .

2. French Sign Language was invented long ago and _____ .

3. Hospitals should _____ and tell the parents the results.

4. Even babies _____ and learn to sign.

5. Parents can teach their babies or _____ .

6. Deaf children _____ and live happier lives with sign language.

7. Family members of deaf children _____ and tell how they feel.

Compound Predicates, continued

B. Use a conjunction from the box to combine the two sentences into one sentence with a compound predicate.

Conjunctions

and

or

8. The word "twin" comes from the German word "twine." The word "twin" means "two together." _The word "twin" comes from the_ _German word "twine" and means "two together."_

9. Identical twins look similar. Identical twins sometimes dress alike. _____

_____

10. Some twins do not look alike. Some twins do not act the same way. _____

_____

11. Identical twins communicate closely. Identical twins share a strong bond. _____

_____

12. Twins gather every year on Twins Day in Twinsburg, Ohio. Twins have fun every year on Twins Day in Twinsburg, Ohio. _____

_____

C. 13.–19. Edit the journal entry below. Combine sentences to create sentences with a compound predicate. Correct any verbs that do not agree with the subject.

Journal Entry

Three years ago I fell. I broke my arm. My grandmother took me to the hospital. My grandmother held my hand. The doctor gave me medicine. The doctor put a cast on my arm. I missed my mother. I felt very sad. At that time I did not know sign language. At that time I could not say how I felt. Now I know sign language. I use it every day. I can use sign language to share my feelings. I can use sign language to tell about my needs.

Revising and Editing Marks

∧	Add.
⤾	Move to here.
∧	Replace with this.
⌿	Take out.
∧	Add a comma.
⊙	Add a period.
≡	Capitalize.
/	Make lower case.

Compound Subjects

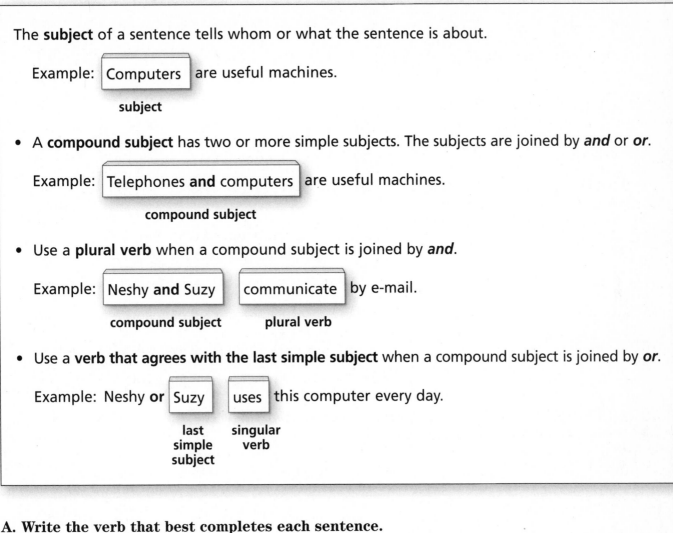

The **subject** of a sentence tells whom or what the sentence is about.

Example: | Computers | are useful machines.
          subject

• A **compound subject** has two or more simple subjects. The subjects are joined by **and** or **or**.

Example: | Telephones **and** computers | are useful machines.
          compound subject

• Use a **plural verb** when a compound subject is joined by **and**.

Example: | Neshy **and** Suzy | | communicate | by e-mail.
          compound subject   plural verb

• Use a **verb that agrees with the last simple subject** when a compound subject is joined by **or**.

Example: Neshy **or** | Suzy | | uses | this computer every day.
                        last   singular
                        simple   verb
                        subject

A. Write the verb that best completes each sentence.

1. Neshy and Suzy _____like_____ playing soccer.
                        like / likes

2. Water skiing and mountain skiing _____ two other sports they like.
                                      are / is

3. Either soccer or individual sports _____ to build character.
                                        help / helps

4. Both Neshy and her sister _____ good soccer players.
                              is / are

5. The twins and their parents _____ the Internet to communicate.
                                use / uses

6. Neshy and Suzy _____ nervous and scared about being separated.
                   are / is

7. Both Neshy and Suzy _____ of having children.
                        dream / dreams

Compound Subjects, continued

B. Neshy and Suzy like to play soccer. Think about sports you like to play. Complete the sentences with the compound subject given in parentheses. Use *and* or *or* to join the simple subjects.

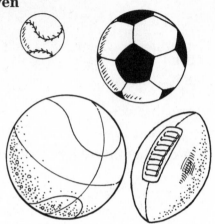

8. _____Baseball and basketball_____ are two of my favorite sports. (**baseball, basketball**)

9. Either _____ is a great place for a baseball game. (**park, field**)

10. _____ are the things I like best about basketball. (**fun, excitement**)

11. _____ come to the games with me. (**friends, family**)

12. Either _____ takes pictures of me in my uniform. (**sister, mom**)

13. _____ talk to me before the game. (**coach, brother**)

14. Either _____ keeps the sun out of my eyes. (**cap, hat**)

15. _____ are my favorite sports teams. (**Bulldogs, Jammers**)

16. _____ takes me to the baseball field. (**mom, neighbor**)

C. 17.–21. Edit the letter below. Make corrections so that the verbs agree with the compound subjects.

Revising and Editing Marks

∧	Add.
↻	Move to here.
⌄	Replace with this.
℘	Take out.
∧	Add a comma.
⊙	Add a period.
≡	Capitalize.
/	Make lower case.

Hi Neshy,

All of your friends and family misses you. My work and my family is keeping me busy. I'm so excited that you will be visiting home soon. Either Monday or Tuesday are a good day to get together. Mom and Dad says that they can come to lunch with us. Our home and our hearts feels empty without you.

See you soon,

Suzy

Adjectives That Compare

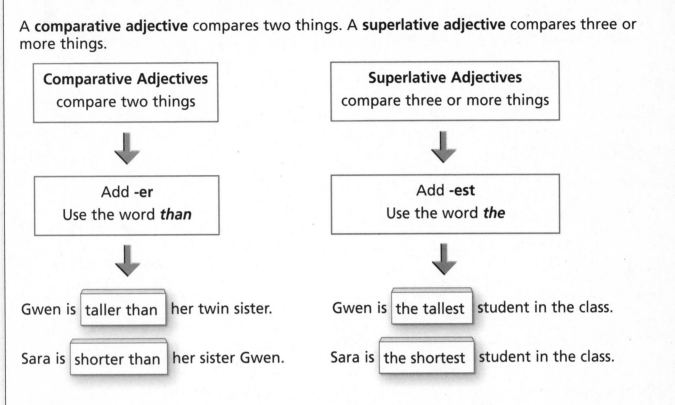

A **comparative adjective** compares two things. A **superlative adjective** compares three or more things.

| **Comparative Adjectives** compare two things | **Superlative Adjectives** compare three or more things |

Add **-er**
Use the word ***than***

Add **-est**
Use the word ***the***

Gwen is | taller than | her twin sister.

Gwen is | the tallest | student in the class.

Sara is | shorter than | her sister Gwen.

Sara is | the shortest | student in the class.

REMEMBER:
- Use ***more*** or ***less*** for long comparative adjectives: **more intelligent, less intelligent**
- Use ***most*** or ***least*** for long superlative adjectives: **the most intelligent, the least intelligent**

A. Circle the correct form of the adjective in each sentence.

1. Sara is _____ (shorter) / shortest _____ than her twin sister Gwen.

2. Sara's test grade was _____ **higher / highest** _____ than Gwen's.

3. Sara's test grade was the _____ **higher / highest** _____ in the class.

4. Gwen is _____ **more athletic / most athletic** _____ than Sara.

5. Gwen thinks that basketball is the _____ **less difficult / least difficult** _____ sport of them all.

6. Sara studies _____ **longer / longest** _____ than her twin sister Gwen.

7. Sara is _____ **more confident / most confident** _____ than her sister about taking the test tomorrow.

8. Gwen is _____ **better / best** _____ than her sister at learning languages.

Adjectives That Compare, continued

B. Use the correct form of the adjective in parentheses to compare the stories "Ginger for the Heart" and "Twins."

ginger

9. "Twins" is a ___more modern___ story than "Ginger for the Heart." (**modern**)

10. "Ginger for the Heart" takes place during an _____ time period than "Twins." (**early**)

11. Yenna's father is the _____ character in the stories. (**old**)

12. In these stories, love is the _____ thing to the characters. (**important**)

13. "Ginger for the Heart" is a _____ story than "Twins." (**interesting**)

14. The _____ event in "Ginger for the Heart" was when the root would not burn. (**surprising**)

15. The _____ time in Maria's life was when she learned her daughters were deaf. (**sad**)

16. Now the twins are _____ than ever before. (**confident**)

signing

C. 17.–22. Edit the letter below. Correct any adjectives that are incorrect.

Dear Neshy and Suzy,

   Your weddings were the more beautiful events I have ever attended. The band was the greater I have heard in a long time. I danced longest than I did at my own wedding! The food was great, too. The salad was delicious than the salad I have for dinner every night. The dinner itself was the more delicious meal I can remember.

Thank you both for inviting me. I can't wait to visit you all again next year. I always have the happier time when I am with you both.

Love,

Aunt Jenna

Revising and Editing Marks	
∧	Add.
⌒	Move to here.
⌐	Replace with this.
℘	Take out.
∧	Add a comma.
⊙	Add a period.
≡	Capitalize.
/	Make lower case.

Skills Review

A. Complete each sentence with an adjective, adverb, or prepositional phrase from the box. Write the kind of word or phrase that is listed in parentheses.

for many years	eventually
from all over the world	several
deeply	often
nimble	

1. As they sat in the tower, Yenna and her mother

   _____often_____ worked long hours sewing garments. (**adverb**)

2. One day Yenna fell _____ in love with a young man who brought garments to be mended. (**adverb**)

3. He would sit and watch her _____ fingers mend his clothes. (**adjective**)

4. The young man went in search of gold with other miners _____ . (**prepositional phrase**)

5. Yenna gave the young man a fragrant ginger root that he saved _____ . (**prepositional phrase**)

6. After years of prospecting for gold, the young man _____ returned to Yenna. (**adverb**)

7. He told her that her gift of the ginger root had saved his life _____ times since he left. (**adjective**)

B. Write an adjective from the box that best fits each sentence.

Some Adjectives

deaf	Mexican
talented	caring
different	happy
double	busy

8. Nesmayda and Suzette are _____deaf_____ twins who communicate with sign language.

9. The _____ twins enjoy many sports, but they excel at playing soccer.

10. The twins watched the _____ team play the German team on television.

11. Having a _____ family helped Nesmayda and Suzette to become independent.

12. The twins were marrried in a _____ ceremony on the same day in 1999.

13. Even though they both have _____ lives, Neshy and Suzy always find time to communicate.

14. The twins spend many _____ hours writing to each other on the Internet.

15. Even though they live in _____ cities, they can still tell each other what is happening in their lives.

Skills Review, continued

C. **Complete the compound predicate in each sentence. Use the correct forms of the verbs in parentheses.**

16. In Chinatown young Bao _____plays_____ outside and _____watches_____ her father in his store. (**play, watch**)

17. As Bao grows up, she _____ hard and _____ the store. (**work, clean**)

18. Bao's mother and father _____ and _____ upstairs above the store. (**eat, sleep**)

19. Bao's two brothers _____ their home and _____ on the railroad. (**leave, work**)

20. Many men _____ in love with Bao and _____ for her hand in marriage. (**fall, ask**)

21. Bao always _____ them down and _____ away. (**turn, walk**)

D. **Circle the compound subject in each sentence. Then complete the sentence with the correct form of the verb in parentheses.**

22. In the story "Ginger for the Heart," (Yenna and her husband) _____use_____ ginger root as a symbol of their love. (**use / uses**)

23. Fresh ginger root and old ginger root _____ different from each other. (**taste / tastes**)

24. Many roots and flowers _____ good food or good medicine. (**make / makes**)

25. Some drinks and a certain kind of candy _____ ginger root. (**contain / contains**)

26. Gingerbread and ginger snaps _____ snacks. (**is / are**)

E. **Complete each sentence. Write the correct form of the comparative or superlative adjective in parentheses.**

27. Neshy uses e-mail because it is _____faster_____ than mail that is hand delivered. (**fast**)

28. Suzy thinks that a computer can be the _____ way to communicate. (**efficient**)

29. Both twins think writing a letter is _____ than sending an e-mail. (**hard**)

30. Talking on a cell phone is sometimes _____ than talking on a telephone in your home. (**expensive**)

31. Speaking to someone in person is the _____ way to communicate. (**personal**)

32. The twins believe typing a letter is _____ than writing a letter by hand. (**slow**)

88

Complex Sentences

A **complex sentence** has an independent clause and a dependent clause.

- The **dependent clause** can come first or last. Use a comma (**,**) after a dependent clause that comes first.

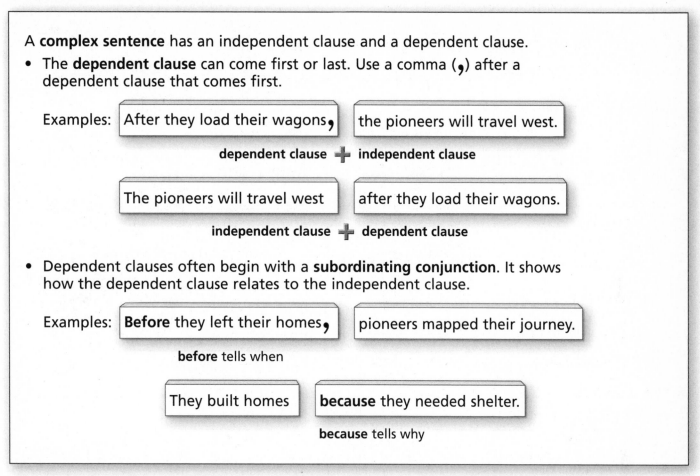

- Dependent clauses often begin with a **subordinating conjunction**. It shows how the dependent clause relates to the independent clause.

A. Choose a subordinating conjunction from the box to complete each complex sentence.

after	although	because	before	until	when	where

1. Early American pioneers traveled west _____when_____ they heard about new opportunities.

2. Pioneers had to choose a trail _____ they could begin their journey.

3. _____ they always traveled with heavy wagons, their journey was difficult.

4. _____ their journey was hard, pioneers still kept traveling.

5. They traveled _____ they found a place to settle.

6. Pioneers settled on flat land _____ they could build houses and farms.

7. _____ the pioneers cleared some land, they built their homes.

8. Pioneers built their homes from sod _____ trees were scarce.

Complex Sentences, continued

B. Combine the sentences to make a complex sentence. Use a subordinating conjunction from the box.

> **Some Subordinating Conjunctions**
>
> | | |
> |---|---|
> | after | since |
> | although | when |
> | because | until |
> | before | where |

9. I enjoy history. I learn about life long ago. _I enjoy history because_

   I learn about life long ago.

10. We studied history. We learned about pioneer wagons. _____

    _____

11. I want to visit St. Louis. Many pioneers began their journey there.

    _____

12. Many pioneers kept detailed journals. Only a few journals have

    been found. _____

    _____

13. The journals were discovered. Many facts about pioneer history were unknown.

    _____

    _____

14. Some journals were passed on to family. A few journals are available at universities

    or museums. _____

    _____

C. Add an independent clause to make a complex sentence.

When we read history books, _____ _we learn more about our ancestors._
                                        15.

_____ because we understand the past better.
                  16.

Unless we learn the lessons of history, _____
                                                        17.

Until I learn more about the pioneers, _____
                                                        18.

_____ if you think your life is hard now.
                  19.

D. 20.–22. Tell a partner about the painting on page 170 of your book. Use three complex sentences with subordinating conjunctions from the box above.

Example: "The little girl is holding on to her mother because she is afraid."

© Hampton-Brown

Complex Sentences

A **complex sentence** has one **independent clause** and one **dependent clause**.

- Dependent clauses begin with a **subordinating conjunction**. It shows how the dependent clause relates to the independent clause.

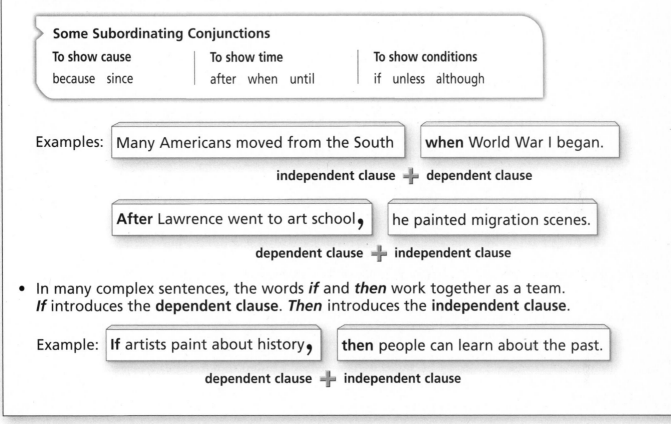

Some Subordinating Conjunctions

To show cause	To show time	To show conditions
because since	after when until	if unless although

Examples: | Many Americans moved from the South | | **when** World War I began. |

independent clause ✛ dependent clause

| **After** Lawrence went to art school, | | he painted migration scenes. |

dependent clause ✛ independent clause

- In many complex sentences, the words *if* and *then* work together as a team. *If* introduces the **dependent clause**. *Then* introduces the **independent clause**.

Example: | **If** artists paint about history, | | **then** people can learn about the past. |

dependent clause ✛ independent clause

A. Use *If* and *then* to combine the two sentences into a complex sentence.

1. People look closely at Jacob Lawrence's paintings. They can learn more about the Great Migration. _If people look closely at Jacob Lawrence's paintings, then they can learn more about the Great Migration._

2. People paint stories. They can express history in different ways. _____

_____

3. A great painting speaks to people. They will appreciate it. _____

_____

4. Great paintings are important to people. They should be in museums. _____

_____

Complex Sentences, continued

B. Write two *if-then* sentences of your own.

5. If _____ ,

   then _____ .

6. If _____ ,

   then _____ .

C. Complete the dependent clause in each sentence. Circle the subordinating conjunction in the clause.

7. (When) _____ people are unhappy, _____ they are more likely to migrate.

8. If _____

   _____ then people would want to move.

9. African Americans moved to the North because _____

   _____ .

10. Jacob Lawrence saw the new hope in African Americans after _____

    _____ .

11. Since _____

    _____ Lawrence painted stories of their history.

12. Before _____

    _____ people did not know much about the Great Migration.

D. 13.–17. Edit the journal entry below. Combine sentences using subordinating conjunctions to create complex sentences.

Journal Entry

March 21, 1916

So many thoughts raced through my head. We were boarding our train to New York.
I am happy to be going. I already miss my home in Georgia. Uncle Willie has probably
received our letter. We sent it weeks ago. We have saved enough money. I would
like to buy some warm blankets. The weather gets cold next winter. We'll have to
buy some warm clothes.

Revising and Editing Marks

∧	Add.
⌒	Move to here.
⌄	Replace with this.
✄	Take out.
∧,	Add a comma.
⊙	Add a period.
≡	Capitalize.
/	Make lower case.

© Hampton-Brown

92

Prepositional Phrases

A **preposition** is a word that shows how a noun or a pronoun connects to other words in a sentence.

Some Prepositions

above	before	for	in	to
after	below	from	on	with

- A **prepositional phrase** begins with a **preposition** and ends with a noun or a pronoun. It includes all the words between the preposition and the noun or pronoun.

Example: The trains were going + *to* a northern city.

prepositional phrase

- Prepositional phrases add details to make writing more interesting.

Examples: They waved goodbye + *from* the train.

prepositional phrase

Their packages were placed + *above* the seats.

prepositional phrase

A. Add prepositional phrases from the box to the sentences.

from the South	in northern factories	with these new workers
for new workers	during World War I	

1. Many workers left their jobs _____ during World War I _____ .

2. There were not enough workers _____ .

3. Factory owners needed new workers _____ .

4. Factory owners bought train tickets _____ .

5. The northbound trains were filled _____ .

Prepositional Phrases, continued

B. Supply details for the following sentences by adding prepositional phrases.

6. Life in the South was difficult _____for African Americans_____ during the war.

7. There was a shortage of workers, and southern farmers had problems _____

   _____.

8. African Americans could get no justice _____.

9. The cotton crop failed and many southern farms were left _____.

10. People wanted to move north _____.

11. Railroad stations were crowded _____.

12. Northern cities grew larger _____.

13. There was a shortage of workers _____.

14. Men were going off to fight _____.

15. Factory owners had to replace them _____.

16. Factory owners lent southern blacks money _____.

C. 17.–23. Revise the letter from a young migrant boy to his friend in the South by correcting each prepositional phrase as needed.

Revising and Editing Marks	
∧	Add.
⌒	Move to here.
⌃	Replace with this.
℘	Take out.
⋏	Add a comma.
⊙	Add a period.
≡	Capitalize.
/	Make lower case.

Dear Samuel,

   We have arrived with the big city. Mom and Dad got jobs in a factory before a few days. The city is so different before back home. I will miss running on the peach trees to the swamp on a hot day. When I moved to the city, I used to sleep with the sound of crickets. In the city, I have to learn to sleep for the hum of factories. However, I am excited about meeting new friends. Dad says we will be going to school above a few weeks. I hope you can visit us soon. I look forward to showing you all the sights of the city.

Your friend,

Willy

Complex Sentences

A **complex sentence** has one **independent clause** and at least one **dependent clause**.

• A **dependent clause** begins with a **subordinating conjunction**.

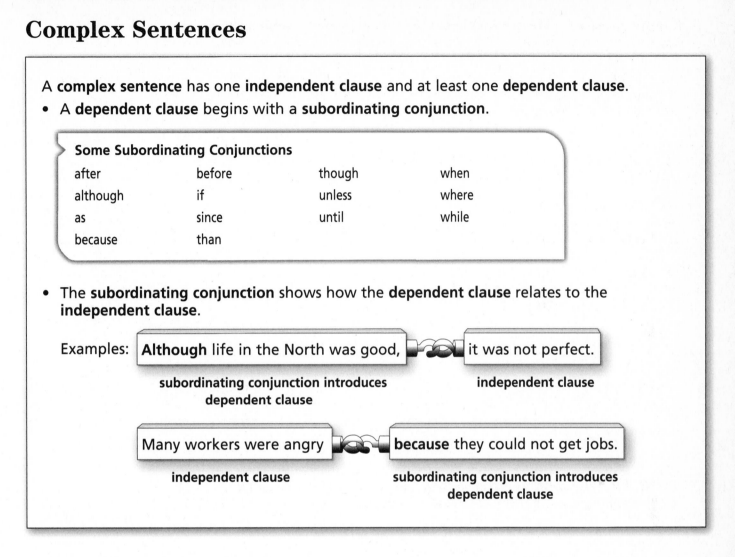

Some Subordinating Conjunctions

after	before	though	when
although	if	unless	where
as	since	until	while
because	than		

• The **subordinating conjunction** shows how the **dependent clause** relates to the **independent clause**.

Examples:

Although life in the North was good, — it was not perfect.

subordinating conjunction introduces dependent clause   independent clause

Many workers were angry — **because** they could not get jobs.

independent clause   subordinating conjunction introduces dependent clause

A. Write a subordinating conjunction from the box above in each sentence.

1. _____ Because _____ segregation ruled the South, black newspapers ran stories about jobs and housing in the North.

2. Agents from northern factories came to the South _____ they needed to find workers.

3. _____ they heard about the jobs, black families gathered to discuss moving north.

4. Railroad stations were crowded with migrants _____ many black families decided to move north.

5. Families moved black children to the North _____ they hoped to find education.

6. _____ they were promised good housing, some families were overcrowded.

Complex Sentences, continued

B. Add a dependent clause to make a complex sentence. Begin each dependent clause with a subordinating conjunction from the box on page 95.

7. People moved north _because they wanted better jobs and education_

_____ .

8. Southern landowners tried to stop migration _____

_____ .

9. Landowners put labor agents in jail _____

_____ .

10. Landowners put migrants in jail _____

_____ .

11. _____ ,

_____ many migrants moved to Pittsburgh.

12. _____ ,

_____ they worked in steel mills.

C. 13.–22. Edit the journal entry below. Combine sentences using subordinating conjunctions to create complex sentences.

Journal Entry

December 16, 1917

I wrap my hands around the cold bars of the jail cell. My stomach hurts. I hear the train whistle in the distance. This train will go north without me. I will be on the next one. Next time, I will not stand on the platform. I can be seen there. I will hide in the coat room. I will be very quiet. I will wait. The train will be ready to leave. Then, I will run and hop on the train. The train will pull away from the station. I will be on my way north. I will find a house. I will be happy. I will finally find freedom. I will have a bright future to look forward to.

Revising and Editing Marks

∧	Add.
⌒	Move to here.
⌃	Replace with this.
႒	Take out.
∧⸴	Add a comma.
⊙	Add a period.
≡	Capitalize.
/	Make lower case.

© Hampton-Brown

Phrases and Clauses

- A **phrase** is a group of words *without* a subject and a verb.

  Example: after school

  prepositional phrase

- A **clause** is a group of words *with* a subject and a verb. An **independent clause** can stand alone as a sentence.

  Example: Jacob Lawrence took art lessons   after school.

  independent clause   **prepositional phrase**

- Two **independent clauses** can form a **compound sentence**. A **coordinating conjunction** such as *and, but,* or *or* can join them.

  Example: Jacob Lawrence took art lessons after school,   **and**   he enjoyed them.

  independent clause ✚ **coordinating** ✚ **independent**
                              conjunction   **clause**

- A **subordinating conjunction** such as *if, when*, or *because* can join a **dependent clause** to an **independent clause** to form a **complex sentence**.

  Example: **Because** Lawrence was an artist,   he painted people and events.

  subordinating   **dependent clause** ✚ **independent clause**
  conjunction

A. Underline the independent clause in the sentence.

1. My family was part of the Great Migration and moved north with other families.

2. Because I was inspired by the Great Migration, I wanted to tell their story in my paintings.

3. Although the Great Migration was about conflict and struggle, I also wanted to celebrate strength and courage.

4. I thought a lot about trains and people walking to the stations.

5. The migration was about movement and I wanted to convey this in my paintings.

Phrases and Clauses, continued

B. Complete the sentences with the type of phrase or clause in parentheses. Choose from the phrases and clauses in the box.

> when he was young
>
> of migrating people
>
> and he found a new subject for his art
>
> he included factory workers in his art
>
> after school

6. Because Lawrence loved art, he took art lessons

   _____ after school _____

   _____ . **(phrase)**

7. _____ , Lawrence moved with his family to New York City. **(dependent clause)**

8. Lawrence's family found a new life in the city, _____

   _____ . **(independent clause)**

9. Lawrence's art is about the struggles and triumphs _____

   _____ . **(phrase)**

10. Because Lawrence thought about field hands leaving farms to work in factories, _____

   _____ . **(independent clause)**

C. 11.–15. Edit the letter below. Make sure that phrases and dependent clauses do not stand alone. Use coordinating and subordinating conjunctions to form compound and complex sentences.

Revising and Editing Marks

∧	Add.
↻	Move to here.
⌐	Replace with this.
˗	Take out.
∧,	Add a comma.
⊙	Add a period.
≡	Capitalize.
/	Make lower case.

Dear Grandma,

Today my class visited the art museum. We saw many interesting and colorful paintings. By the artist Jacob Lawrence. He painted scenes of people and events. From the Great Migration. Although the paintings had bold colors such as red and blue. There were also dark colors such as black and brown. The people in the paintings looked as if they were built from shapes. Because I saw circles, squares, and triangles inside each person. There was also a lot of energy in the paintings. And there was a lot of hope.

Love,

Maria

Indefinite Adjectives

An **indefinite adjective** tells "about how many" or "about how much." It does not tell the exact number or amount.

> **Some Indefinite Adjectives**
>
> | How Many | | How Much | | |
> |---|---|---|---|---|
> | a few | several | a little | not much | much |
> | many | some | a lot | some | |

- When you know exactly how many, you can use a number word.

  Example: **Two** Underground Railroad conductors were Harriet Tubman and Peg Leg Joe.

- When you do not know the exact number or amount, you can use an **indefinite adjective**.

  Examples: They helped **many** slaves escape to the North.

  indefinite adjective

  Some of the escaped slaves were captured and returned to the South.

  indefinite adjective

A. Add indefinite adjectives from the box above to the sentences.

1. _____Many_____ people felt sympathy for the slaves.

2. _____ people were brave enough to help them.

3. Underground Railroad conductors risked their lives to provide slaves with

   _____ help.

4. _____ slave owners offered rewards for the return of slaves.

5. _____ people allowed slaves to hide in their basements or barns.

6. _____ is known about the songs that helped slaves to find a way north.

7. These songs contained _____ clues about paths to the North.

8. With _____ planning, slaves were able to travel the path to freedom.

Indefinite Adjectives, continued

B. Complete each sentence with an indefinite adjective that fits the label in parentheses.

9. The Underground Railroad journey was so difficult that _____ some _____ escaped slaves wanted to turn back. (**how many**)

10. There were not _____ rafts or boats, so the slaves had to swim across the rivers. (**how many**)

11. A successful trip north required _____ of luck and courage. (**how much**)

12. The slaves traveled without _____ supplies. (**how many**)

13. When the slaves reached an Underground conductor, they knew there was

    _____ farther to go. (**how much**)

14. There were _____ miles of connecting rivers to cross. (**how many**)

15. The fugitive slaves endured _____ hardship. (**how much**)

16. _____ slaves who reached the North could look forward to a safe, new home. (**how many**)

C. 17.–22. Edit the letter below by replacing the exact numbers or amounts with indefinite adjectives.

Revising and Editing Marks

∧	Add.
⌒	Move to here.
⌒	Replace with this.
⌿	Take out.
⌄	Add a comma.
⊙	Add a period.
≡	Capitalize.
/	Make lower case.

Dear Aunt Sofia,

Today my parents took my sisters and me to see the Underground Railroad museum in Cincinnati, Ohio. There are only one or two museums like it in the country. The museum sits on the banks of the Ohio River. This is where about one thousand escaped slaves entered the free state of Ohio on their way to Canada. Ohio was one of about eighteen free states or territories before the Civil War. Inside the museum, I visited two or three slave pens, and I saw about seven posters offering rewards for escaped slaves. I also saw four or five movies about slavery and the Underground Railroad. In one area, there was a wall filled with about a thousand messages held by magnets. The messages on the wall gave me hope for the future. I added my own message to the wall: To stay free, help others to live free.

Love, Consuelo

Helping Verbs

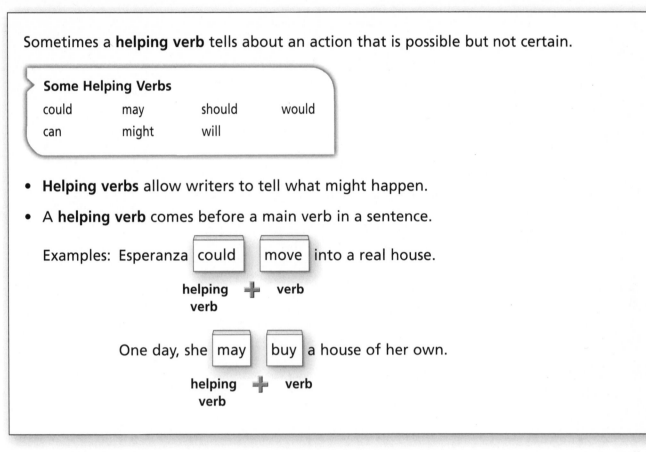

Sometimes a **helping verb** tells about an action that is possible but not certain.

Some Helping Verbs

could	may	should	would
can	might	will	

- **Helping verbs** allow writers to tell what might happen.

- A **helping verb** comes before a main verb in a sentence.

Examples: Esperanza could move into a real house.

helping + verb
verb

One day, she may buy a house of her own.

helping + verb
verb

A. Add helping verbs to the sentences below.

1. When Esperanza grows up, she _____ **may** _____ buy a large house.

2. She _____ like a house with real stairs.

3. Her dream house _____ have a basement.

4. She _____ like a house with three bathrooms.

5. The house _____ have a big yard and some trees.

6. Her father _____ buy a lottery ticket when he is at the store.

7. Her mother _____ dream about the new house all day.

8. Esperanza _____ remember the stories her mother told her.

9. The whole family _____ like to move to a nice house.

10. Esperanza's family _____ continue to dream about moving.

11. One day their dream _____ come true.

Helping Verbs, continued

B. In the letter below, fill in the details using helping verbs.

CAN I BUILD YOUR DREAM HOME?
Do you want stairs? Do you want a basement?
Tell me what you want. I can design it!
Call or write today.

Dear Ms. Builder:

My name is Esperanza. Today I live on Mango Street, but Mango Street is not where

I belong. One day I _____**may**_____ live on the other side of town. My house is small
                          12.

and red. I do not like it very much. Perhaps you _____ build my dream
                                                        13.

house. First, I _____ need pipes that work so that I _____
                      14.   **15.**

have running water throughout the house. I am not sure, but I _____
                                                                        16.

need a wide staircase in the middle of the house, just like the ones I see on TV. Next,

I _____ need a basement for storage and laundry. Finally, the house
        17.

_____ include a big yard. Please let me know whether you can help me
        18.

build my dream house.

Sincerely, Esperanza

C. 19.–24. Edit the letter below by adding helping verbs.

Dear Esperanza:

Thank you for your letter. I appreciate your interest in my design work. I want

to work with you. First, I draw some sample houses. Then, I ask you to look at the

sample drawings. Next, you tell me what you like and what you don't like. I change

the drawings based on your ideas. I hope that we find a design you like.

Sincerely, Ms. Builder

Revising and Editing Marks

∧   Add.
↻   Move to here.
⌃   Replace with this.
✓   Take out.
⌄   Add a comma.
⊙   Add a period.
≡   Capitalize.
/   Make lower case.

Two-Word Verbs

Some verbs are two-word verbs. They are made up of a verb and a small word such as *by, in,* or *out*.

> **Some Two-Word Verbs**
>
> | | | | |
> |---|---|---|---|
> | break down | give up | pass up | turn in |
> | get ahead | look forward | run into | turn off |
> | get out | look over | run out | |
> | get over | pass by | stand for | |
> | give out | pass out | stand out | |

• The meaning of the **two-word verb** is different from the verb by itself.

Examples: A teacher ⎡ passed ⎤ me a notebook.

meaning: hand from one to another

I ⎡ passed by ⎤ the library on my way home.

meaning: go near or move in front of

A. Choose the correct word to make a two-word verb in each sentence. Use the list of two-word verbs and their meanings on Handbook pages 452–453 to help you.

1. Esperanza passed _____ out _____ a copy of her latest story to her friends.

out / up

2. Esperanza passed _____ the rice in favor of the potatoes.

for / up

3. If Esperanza studies hard, she feels she will get _____ in life.

ahead / out

4. Esperanza would like to get _____ of the house on Mango Street some day.

ahead / out

5. Esperanza will turn _____ one of her stories for a class assignment.

in / off

6. Esperanza is glad there is no landlord on Mango Street to turn _____ the water in

   the pipes.

over / off

Two-Word Verbs, continued

**B. Which two-word verb goes with the meaning of the sentence?
Write it in the sentence.**

stand out	get out	run out	give up	break down	look forward

7. Esperanza was afraid they would _____run out_____ of hot water when she lived on Loomis Street.

8. Esperanza hopes that the washing machine doesn't _____ before the end of the school year.

9. It is so hot inside the house on Mango Street that she has to _____ to breathe some fresh air.

10. Esperanza is quiet and she doesn't like to _____ in a crowd.

11. If Esperanza's family doesn't move soon, she may _____ all hope.

12. Esperanza and her family _____ to the day they will move from Mango Street.

C. 13.–18. Edit the journal entry below by correcting the two-word verbs.

Journal Entry

Dear Diary,

I was so embarrassed today. One of the nuns from my school passed up my house on

Mango Street. She asked me where I lived. I pointed to my house. I know my house

stands by because of the crumbling bricks and tiny yard. The nun quickly looked

ahead the front of the house with its peeling paint and wooden bars on the windows.

She wrinkled her nose and made her voice sound funny when she said, "There?" Oh, Diary, I

didn't think I could get by the embarrassment! Mama and Papa promised that we would find

a good house, but this house on Mango Street isn't it. It's awful! I just have to give out of

this house! When I go to school tomorrow, I will walk the long way to science class. I don't

want to run out that nun. I hope that I never see her again.

Revising and Editing Marks

∧	Add.
⟳	Move to here.
∧	Replace with this.
⟋	Take out.
∧	Add a comma.
⊙	Add a period.
≡	Capitalize.
╱	Make lower case.

© Hampton-Brown

Complex Sentences

A **complex sentence** has one **independent clause** and one or more **dependent clauses**.

- The dependent clause may begin with the **subordinating conjunction** *because* or *since*. It answers a question about why.

Examples: Why did you quit school?

| I quit school | | *because* I didn't have nice clothes. |

independent clause ✚ dependent clause

| *Since* I didn't have nice clothes, | | I quit school. |

dependent clause ✚ independent clause

A. Make complex sentences. Choose a dependent clause from the box that makes sense with each independent clause.

because she likes to sing	Since Esperanza's mother likes to draw
because she wants Esperanza to listen	because she can speak two languages
because she quit school	Since Esperanza's mother was not able to finish school

1. Esperanza's mother says that she could have been somebody <u>because she can speak two</u>

   <u>languages</u> .

2. _____ ,

   _____ Esperanza's mother learned to draw with needle and thread.

3. Esperanza's mother borrows opera records from the public library _____

   _____ .

4. Esperanza's mother taps a wooden spoon on the table _____

   _____ .

5. _____ ,

   _____ she tells Esperanza to go to school and study hard.

Complex Sentences, continued

B. Answer the questions below with complex sentences. Use the subordinating conjunction *because* or *since*.

6. Why does Esperanza think that the trees understand her?

Esperanza thinks that the trees understand her because they
are skinny, pointy, and misplaced.

7. Why doesn't Nenny appreciate the trees?

_____

_____

8. Why are the trees strong? _____

_____

9. Why does Esperanza admire the trees? _____

_____

10. Why does Esperanza look at the trees? _____

_____

11. Why do the trees remind Esperanza of tulips? _____

_____

C. 12.–21. Edit the journal entry below by combining short sentences to form complex sentences. Use the subordinating conjunction *because* or *since* to introduce dependent clauses.

Journal Entry

October 22

My mother wants me to stay in school. She wants me to be somebody. She quit

school. She feels as if she's nobody. I admire my mother so much, however. She

sings, sews, and takes care of me. She has high hopes for me. I don't want her to

know that I sometimes feel sad and skinny. My mother says that she let shame ruin

her life. I do not want the same thing to happen to me. The trees keep keeping. I know

that I can, too.

Revising and Editing Marks

∧	Add.
⤸	Move to here.
⌢	Replace with this.
͜	Take out.
∧	Add a comma.
⊙	Add a period.
≡	Capitalize.
/	Make lower case.

Skills Review

A. Choose the subordinating conjunction that best completes each complex sentence.

1. Esperanza wants a house of her own _____when_____ she grows up.
   <u>when / if</u>

2. _____ she lived in a lot of different houses, Esperanza moved to Mango Street.
   <u>After / Because</u>

3. Esperanza tells stories of her life _____ she moved to Mango Street.
   <u>since / while</u>

4. Her family moved a lot _____ they didn't own a house.
   <u>because / until</u>

5. Esperanza dreams of a better life _____ she finishes school.
   <u>after / although</u>

6. _____ it's not the house she dreamed of, Esperanza is happy that her
   <u>Although / Since</u>
   family owns it.

B. Choose a preposition and use it to write a prepositional phrase to complete the sentence.

7. Esperanza didn't always live _____on Mango Street_____.
   <u>on / to</u>

8. Before Mango Street, they lived _____.
   <u>in / over</u>

9. Esperanza dreams of a big house _____.
   <u>for / with</u>

10. Her parents also dream _____.
    <u>of / near</u>

11. Esperanza's mother wants her to go _____.
    <u>to / after</u>

12. She knows she has to work hard _____.
    <u>for / during</u>

13. Esperanza will continue to write stories _____.
    <u>about / from</u>

14. She will be a famous writer _____.
    <u>in / at</u>

15. Esperanza will help people _____.
    <u>near / from</u>

16. Esperanza will then return home _____.
    <u>to / on</u>

Skills Review, continued

C. In each sentence, write an indefinite adjective that can replace the word or words below the blank.

Indefinite Adjectives

many / much

some

a little / a few

several

17. _____Many_____ people consider Harriet Tubman a hero.
    Millions of

18. Not _____ information is known about Harriet
    a large amount of
    Tubman's early life.

19. She escaped slavery _____ years after she married.
    approximately five

20. There were _____ routes for the Underground Railroad.
    around thirteen

21. Harriet Tubman worked with _____ other people to help slaves escape.
    around four

22. The escaping slaves passed _____ rivers.
    at least three

23. The slaves who escaped had _____ hope for a better future.
    a medium amount of

D. Write a helping verb to complete each of the sentences.

Helping Verbs

could

would

should

may

might

will

24. You _____could_____ think of a house in many ways.

25. Some people _____ consider it just a place to live.

26. Others _____ think it represents their future.

27. Many _____ move to a bigger house when their family grows.

28. People _____ move to find better opportunities.

29. Although moving _____ be difficult, there are also positive benefits.

30. It _____ be wise to move in the summer, while school is out.

E. Write the two-word verb from the box that best fits each sentence.

Two-Word Verbs

give up = abandon

give out = run out

get through = survive, endure

get ahead = succeed, advance

31. You will _____get ahead_____ if you work hard.

32. Some people _____ their dreams too quickly.

33. Your strength will not _____ if you remain hopeful.

34. You can _____ your hard times.

35. When you _____ in life, you can help others.

36. Don't _____ now, because others need your help.

© Hampton-Brown

Skills Review and Practice Tests

A. Write the correct form of the adjective in parentheses.

1. The _____greatest_____ discovery in the history of California happened in 1847. (**great**)

2. A man working near the American River saw something that was _____ than a drop of sunlight. (**bright**)

3. It was a tiny piece of gold, _____ than a pea. (**small**)

4. Yet this discovery led to the _____ event in the West. (**exciting**)

5. Thousands of people rushed to California _____ way they could. (**quick**)

6. These gold miners dreamed of becoming _____ than a king. (**rich**)

7. Each dream seemed to be _____ than the next. (**wild**)

8. The _____ man in the Gold Rush didn't look for gold, though. (**rich**)

9. He was _____ than the gold miners. (**practical**)

10. He sold shovels, the _____ thing the miners needed. (**important**)

B. Complete each sentence. Write the correct preposition.

11. During the Gold Rush, it was difficult to get _____to_____ California.
    <u>above / to</u>

12. Some people traveled _____ wagons.
    <u>in / of</u>

13. The journey _____ America was long and hard.
    <u>across / before</u>

14. The trip could last _____ six months.
    <u>for / on</u>

15. Getting to California _____ ship was difficult, too.
    <u>before / by</u>

16. One sea route went _____ the tip of South America.
    <u>with / around</u>

17. Travelers dreamed _____ gold on the long, dangerous journey.
    <u>after / about</u>

18. The motion _____ the sea often made them sick.
    <u>of / to</u>

19. Insects crawled _____ the food, and the water was not fresh.
    <u>of / in</u>

20. People were probably filled _____ joy when they arrived in California.
    <u>below / with</u>

C. Read the passage. Read each item carefully. Choose the best answer. Mark your answer.

The California Gold Rush of 1849 began a population boom for the state of California. It was a period of history that saw the first large migration of people into California. When gold was first discovered <u>on the river banks</u> in
1
Northern California, migrants came from all over the world to find riches. People came from as far away as Europe, Asia, and South America. By 1850, the mining country had become quite populated. Some miners were <u>lucky</u> than others.
2
Many miners did not find any gold but decided to stay in California and start businesses. With dreams of a better future, the migrants made the most of the skills they had. Many migrants started selling goods <u>in the gold miners</u>.
3
Some began farming where there was good soil—some regions had <u>richest</u> soil than others.
4
Some migrants were recruited to help extract other metals and minerals <u>with the mines</u>. The
5
migrants also provided labor for a new railway system to promote the growth of the state.

Since the Gold Rush, California has grown rapidly and now has the <u>large</u> population of all
6
the states in the United States.

21. In number 1, which of these is the preposition?
- Ⓐ on
- Ⓑ the
- Ⓒ river
- Ⓓ banks

22. In number 2, lucky is best written —
- Ⓕ lucker
- Ⓖ luckier
- Ⓗ most lucky
- Ⓙ as it is written

23. In number 3, in the gold miners is best written —
- Ⓐ to the gold miners
- Ⓑ by the gold miners
- Ⓒ on the gold miners
- Ⓓ as it is written

24. In number 4, richest is best written —
- Ⓕ rich
- Ⓖ richer
- Ⓗ most rich
- Ⓙ as it is written

25. In number 5, with the mines is best written —
- Ⓐ to the mines
- Ⓑ from the mines
- Ⓒ since the mines
- Ⓓ as it is written

26. In number 6, large is best written —
- Ⓕ largest
- Ⓖ larger
- Ⓗ most large
- Ⓙ as it is written

Skills Review and Practice Tests, continued

D. Choose the correct subordinating conjunction to complete each sentence.

27. Jacob Lawrence became famous _____because_____ his "Migration" paintings were so
    before / because

    powerful.

28. These paintings told stories of a time in U.S. history _____ many African
    when / if

    Americans were moving north to find a better future.

29. _____ all good painters work well with colors and shapes, the best tell
    Although / When

    powerful stories in their pictures.

30. The Mexican artist Diego Rivera painted scenes of industrial life _____
    because / so that

    he wanted to tell stories about working people.

31. _____ he traveled to the U.S., Rivera studied history, politics, and art.
    Before/ Where

32. Grandma Moses is also famous for telling stories with her pictures _____
    although / if

    she painted mostly about country life.

33. Grandma Moses was seventy-six years old _____ she became famous
    as if / when

    for her paintings that told important stories about the past.

E. Complete the dependent clause to form a complex sentence.

34. I think some artists become famous **because** ____they have talent and work hard____ .

35. An art gallery is a place **where** _____ .

36. I like paintings **when** _____ .

37. **If** _____ ,

    _____ then it would be fun to be an artist.

38. I know about some African American artists **because** _____

    _____ .

39. I need to learn more **before** _____ .

F. **Read the passage. Read each item carefully. Choose the best answer. Mark your answer.**

Jacob Lawrence was born in 1917 and is one of the most famous African American artists of the twentieth century. His family migrated to the North <u>until he was born</u>. His parents were part of
$\overline{\qquad 1 \qquad}$
the Great Migration of African Americans from the rural South to the urban North that took place in the early twentieth century.

His art was first noticed in Harlem <u>if he was a teenager</u>. In 1941, he completed the
$\overline{\qquad 2 \qquad}$
Migration Series. This was a series of sixty paintings. The paintings show images of the Great Migration. The series was featured in a popular magazine and he quickly became well-known. <u>Lawrence became famous. He started painting historical portraits</u>. He did several famous people.
$\overline{\qquad\qquad 3 \qquad\qquad}$
One of his subjects was Harriet Tubman. <u>Lawrence painted people. He wanted to tell their stories</u>.
$\overline{\qquad\qquad 4 \qquad\qquad}$
In 1990, he was awarded the United States National Medal of the Arts for his contribution to American art. <u>After he settled in Seattle</u>, Lawrence taught at the University of Washington for many
$\overline{\qquad 5 \qquad}$
years. Lawrence died in 2000 after he enjoyed a long career as an artist.

40. In number 1, <u>until he was born</u> is best written —
- Ⓐ if he was born
- Ⓑ unless he was born
- Ⓒ before he was born
- Ⓓ as it is written

41. In number 2, <u>if he was a teenager</u> is best written —
- Ⓕ until he was a teenager
- Ⓖ since he was a teenager
- Ⓗ when he was a teenager
- Ⓙ as it is written

42. The best way to combine the sentences in number 3 is —
- Ⓐ After Lawrence became famous, he started painting historical portraits.
- Ⓑ If Lawrence became famous, he started painting historical portraits.
- Ⓒ Although Lawrence became famous, he started painting historical portraits.
- Ⓓ The sentences cannot be combined.

43. The best way to combine the sentences in number 4 is —
- Ⓕ Lawrence painted people if he wanted to tell their stories.
- Ⓖ Lawrence painted people after he wanted to tell their stories.
- Ⓗ Lawrence painted people because he wanted to tell their stories.
- Ⓙ Lawrence painted people although he wanted to tell their stories.

44. In number 5, <u>After he settled in Seattle</u> is best written —
- Ⓐ If he settled in Seattle
- Ⓑ Unless he settled in Seattle
- Ⓒ Although he settled in Seattle
- Ⓓ as it is written

112

Relative Clauses

A **relative clause** is a dependent clause in a complex sentence. It tells about a noun or a pronoun.

- A **relative pronoun** begins a relative clause.

Relative Pronouns

Use for People	Use for Groups or Things
who	that
whom	which
whose	

Examples:

Many people	**who** visit Greece	see old temples and the Acropolis.

relative   relative
pronoun   clause

The temples are monuments	**that** the ancient Greeks built.

relative   relative
pronoun   clause

The Acropolis is a hilltop,	**which** contains many ancient ruins.

relative   relative
pronoun   clause

A. Circle the relative pronoun in each sentence. Underline the relative clause.

1. The hillside has streets (that) lead up to the Acropolis.

2. The gateway to the Acropolis is the Propylaea, which was built around 432 B.C.E.

3. This gateway kept out people who were not allowed to enter.

4. Mnesikles was the architect who designed the Propylaea.

5. The Propylaea has a center building and two wings that are on the sides of the central building.

6. The north wing had stone walls, which had painted panels.

7. There were more beautiful paintings that covered the ceiling.

Relative Clauses, continued

B. Use a relative clause from the box to complete each sentence.

which is now a museum
that are not in ruins
which can be very slippery
that are held in the theater of Herod Atticus
who know the area

8. Some ancient buildings ___that are not in ruins___

_____ are still used today.

9. Tour guides _____

_____ will take you sightseeing.

10. You can go to concerts _____

_____ .

11. A building called the Stoa of Attalos, _____ ,

_____ has many ancient treasures in it.

12. The Areopagos rock has steps, _____

_____ , carved into it.

C. Read about this school building. Add a relative clause to each sentence to tell about the building.

13. The outside walls, ___which are made of brick___ , look very strong.

14. The parking lot _____ is long and wide.

15. The row of parking spaces is for the buses _____ .

16. The inside walls are painted green, _____ .

17. The cafeteria has tables _____ .

18. The stairs, _____ , are at the ends of the building.

19. Students _____ take good care of the building.

D. 20.–22. Tell a partner about the illustration of the Parthenon on page 216 of your book. Use relative clauses in your sentences.

Example: "The Parthenon, which is an ancient building, is near Athens."

114

Relative Clauses

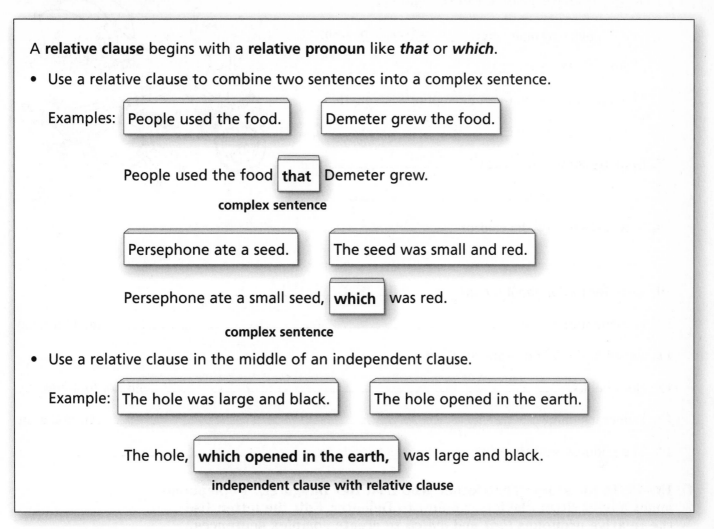

A **relative clause** begins with a **relative pronoun** like *that* or *which*.

- Use a relative clause to combine two sentences into a complex sentence.

Examples: | People used the food. | | Demeter grew the food. |

People used the food | that | Demeter grew.

complex sentence

| Persephone ate a seed. | | The seed was small and red. |

Persephone ate a small seed, | which | was red.

complex sentence

- Use a relative clause in the middle of an independent clause.

Example: | The hole was large and black. | | The hole opened in the earth. |

The hole, | which opened in the earth, | was large and black.

independent clause with relative clause

A. Use *which* and *that* to combine the two sentences into a complex sentence.

1. In the myths, three main gods ruled the world. The Greeks created the myths. _In the myths, which_

    the Greeks created, three main gods ruled the world.

2. Zeus ruled the sky from Mount Olympus. Mount Olympus is the highest mountain in Greece.

    _____

    _____

3. Zeus's brother Poseidon had a kingdom. His kingdom was in the sea. _____

    _____

4. Their brother Hades ruled the underworld. The underworld kept all of the dead. _____

    _____

Relative Clauses, continued

**B. Add a relative clause to complete each sentence.
Circle the relative pronoun in the clause.**

5. The Greeks had many myths ___(that) explained why___

___things happened___.

6. The story of Demeter and Persephone is a myth

_____.

7. Demeter grew trees _____

_____.

8. A swineherd saw the chariot _____

_____.

9. Demeter forgot about the crops _____.

10. Persephone's voice, _____, seemed far away.

11. Persephone did not want the food _____.

12. Her cheeks, _____, did not look healthy.

13. Demeter's hair, _____, turned gray.

14. The goddess was so sad _____.

C. 15.–19. In the story "The Mother Who Lost Her Daughter," Persephone
might have written the letter below to Demeter. Edit the letter. Use
the relative pronouns *that* and *which* to create complex sentences.

Dear Mother,

    Hades drove a chariot. It was very fast. You could not have chased it. There

was a hole in the earth. The hole has closed now. I cannot get out of here. Now I sit

on a throne. The throne is hard and cold. I dream about the meadow. The meadow is

full of pretty flowers. Your face is always on my mind. I long to see your face.

Your loving daughter,

Persephone

Revising and Editing Marks

∧	Add.
↶	Move to here.
↖	Replace with this.
৭	Take out.
∧̣	Add a comma.
⊙	Add a period.
≡	Capitalize.
/	Make lower case.

© Hampton-Brown

Name _____   Date _____

Relative Clauses

A **relative clause** begins with a **relative pronoun**. The relative pronoun connects a relative clause to a noun or pronoun in the sentence.

- Use the relative pronoun *that* for people or things.

- Use the relative pronouns *who* or *whose* for people.

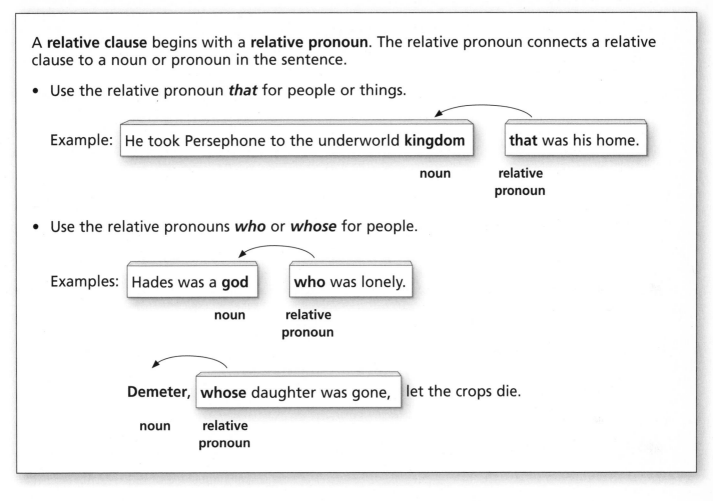

Example: He took Persephone to the underworld **kingdom**   **that** was his home.

noun   relative pronoun

Examples: Hades was a **god**   **who** was lonely.

noun   relative pronoun

Demeter, **whose** daughter was gone, let the crops die.

noun   relative pronoun

A. Choose a relative pronoun from the box to complete each sentence.

| that   who   whose |

1. Long ago the humans _____who_____ lived on Earth did not have fire.

2. The caves _____ they lived in were always dark.

3. Prometheus was a god _____ cared about the humans.

4. He gave them gifts _____ made their lives easier.

5. Prometheus gave them fire _____ Zeus gave only to the gods.

6. The people _____ lives got better were very happy.

7. Zeus was angry with Prometheus, _____ had disobeyed him.

8. He gave Prometheus a punishment _____ lasted for many years.

© Hampton-Brown

Relative Clauses, continued

B. Complete each sentence with a relative clause. Begin the clause with
who, whose, **or** *that.*

9. Aruna, _____ who lives in California _____ ,
   enjoys fruits that grow in each season of the year.

10. In the fall, she likes the apples _____ .

11. She makes pies from pumpkins _____ .

12. In the winter, she eats pomegranates _____
    _____ .

13. Her mother, _____ ,
    _____ makes cranberry bread.

14. She gives cranberry bread to her neighbors, _____
    _____ .

15. In the spring, she gets oranges _____
    _____ .

16. She shares the oranges with her friends, _____ .

17. In the summer, she gets peaches from a farmer _____ .

18. Aruna's brother, _____ , brings tomatoes to the family.

**C. 19.–23. Edit the journal entry below. Use the correct relative pronouns
in the sentences.**

Journal Entry

A Winter Day, Many Years Ago

It is so cold and dark now! Demeter, that used to grow our food, has forgotten us.

She is always looking for Persephone, that has gone to the underworld. Our crops,

who used to be so plentiful, are all dead. Zeus should punish Hades, that selfishness

caused our problems. These gods, whose want us to honor them, do not treat the

humans very well.

Revising and Editing Marks

∧	Add.
⟳	Move to here.
⟍	Replace with this.
ℓ	Take out.
⋏	Add a comma.
⊙	Add a period.
≡	Capitalize.
/	Make lower case.

© Hampton-Brown

Adverbs

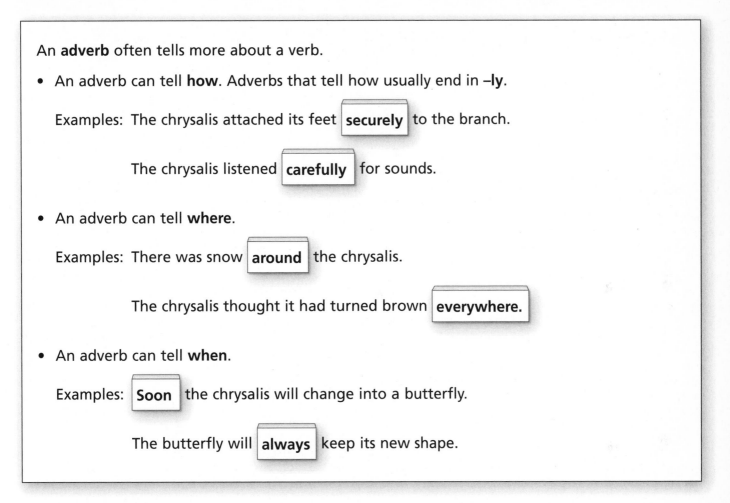

An **adverb** often tells more about a verb.

- An adverb can tell **how**. Adverbs that tell how usually end in **–ly**.

  Examples: The chrysalis attached its feet securely to the branch.

  The chrysalis listened carefully for sounds.

- An adverb can tell **where**.

  Examples: There was snow around the chrysalis.

  The chrysalis thought it had turned brown everywhere.

- An adverb can tell **when**.

  Examples: Soon the chrysalis will change into a butterfly.

  The butterfly will always keep its new shape.

A. Choose an adverb from the box to complete each sentence.

nearby	now	often	skillfully	soon	underground	violently	when

1. The ancient Romans did not understand the volcanoes that erupted _____violently_____ in their country.

2. They could _____ see fire and smoke from Mount Etna.

3. People who lived _____ made up a story about the volcano.

4. They said that the god Vulcan lived _____ .

5. Vulcan was a blacksmith who _____ made things for the other gods.

6. _____ Vulcan used his tools, fire and dust flew from the mountain.

7. People _____ gave the name "volcano" to this type of erupting mountain.

8. People _____ know what really causes volcanoes.

B. Add details to the sentences. Include the kind of adverb shown below each sentence.

9. Some volcanoes erupt ___suddenly___ (how).

10. They may be quiet for years but then ____________ (how) erupt.

11. The eruption starts ____________ (where).

12. The pressure on the water in a volcano may build ____________ (how).

13. ____________ (when) the pressure is taken away, the water turns to steam.

14. The earth starts to shake ____________ (how).

15. Blasts of steam may shoot out of the opening ____________ (where).

16. People who are ____________ (where) must move to safety.

17. Airplane pilots cannot see ____________ (how) through the smoke and ash.

18. There can be a lot of damage ____________ (where).

C. 19.–24. Edit the journal entry below. Add adverbs that tell more about the verbs.

Journal Entry

May 19, 1980

My family and I lived about 60 miles from Mount St. Helens at the time of the eruption. We were watching the eruption on television. It became too dangerous for the camera crews. They all left the area. I looked out my living room window. All of the cars on the street were coated with gray ash. I put some of the ash in a little bottle. I still have that bottle to remind me of the eruption.

Revising and Editing Marks

Mark	Meaning
∧	Add.
⌒	Move to here.
∧	Replace with this.
℘	Take out.
∧,	Add a comma.
⊙	Add a period.
≡	Capitalize.
/	Make lower case.

© Hampton-Brown

Relative Clauses

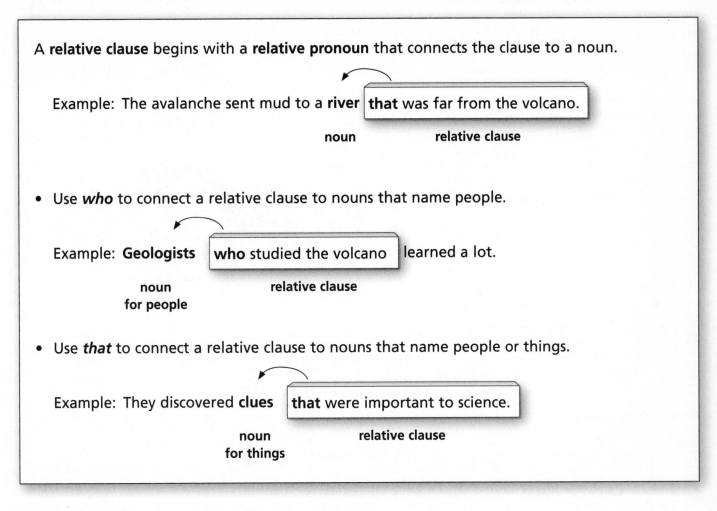

A **relative clause** begins with a **relative pronoun** that connects the clause to a noun.

Example: The avalanche sent mud to a **river** | **that** was far from the volcano.

                                         noun   **relative clause**

- Use **who** to connect a relative clause to nouns that name people.

Example: **Geologists** | **who** studied the volcano | learned a lot.

               noun   **relative clause**
               for people

- Use **that** to connect a relative clause to nouns that name people or things.

Example: They discovered **clues** | **that** were important to science.

                       noun   **relative clause**
                    for things

A. Read each sentence. Circle the correct relative pronoun.

1. Mount St. Helens is a volcano _____ who /(that)_____ has erupted several times.

2. In 1980, people _____ who / that _____ lived nearby had to leave their homes for a while.

3. Many of the plants _____ who / that _____ grew on the mountain were destroyed.

4. Some animals _____ who / that _____ ran away later came back.

5. Mud _____ who / that _____ flowed from the volcano damaged the land.

6. The rushing mud carried away houses _____ who / that _____ were in its path.

7. Some people _____ who / that _____ escaped lost their houses.

8. After the eruption, the mountain had a new shape _____ who / that _____ looked very different.

9. The clues are important for the scientists _____ who / that _____ study them.

10. The clues help predict things _____ who / that _____ might happen again.

Relative Clauses, continued

B. Write sentences about "The Big Blast." Use relative clauses and the relative pronouns *that* and *who*.

11. The volcano _that erupted caused a lot of damage_

_____ .

12. The smoke _____

_____ .

13. The forests _____

_____ .

14. The people _____

_____ .

15. The new crater _____

_____ .

16. The scientists _____

_____ .

17. They search for clues _____

_____ .

C. 18.–22. Edit the letter below. Make sure the relative pronouns are used correctly.

Revising and Editing Marks

∧	Add.
↶	Move to here.
↖	Replace with this.
ɣ	Take out.
∧	Add a comma.
⊙	Add a period.
≡	Capitalize.
/	Make lower case.

May 17

Dear Jeff,

   I'm here at Mount St. Helens, the volcano who erupted in 1980. Now there is a

visitors' center with guides whose talk about the eruption. There are many pictures

who show the damage. The deck, who looks out over the valley, is a good viewing

place. I saw a herd of elk whose had come back to live here again.

Best regards,

Antonio

© Hampton-Brown

Skills Review

A. Choose the relative pronoun that best completes each complex sentence.

1. The chrysalis, _____which_____ hung on the branch, turned into a butterfly.
   <u>which / who</u>

2. It missed the green leaves _____ had disappeared.
   <u>whose / that</u>

3. The wind _____ blew shook the chrysalis.
   <u>who / that</u>

4. The chrysalis liked to see the snowflakes _____ fell all around it.
   <u>whose / that</u>

5. The man _____ wrote the poem watched the seasons change.
   <u>who / that</u>

6. Paul Fleischman is a poet _____ ideas sometimes come from the world around him.
   <u>that / whose</u>

7. He moved to the state of New Hampshire, _____ influenced his writing.
   <u>which / who</u>

8. The sounds of nature, _____ he heard all around him, drifted into his poetry.
   <u>which / that</u>

B. Use _which_ and _that_ to combine the two sentences into a complex sentence.

9. Mount St. Helens is in Washington. Mount St. Helens is an active volcano. _Mount St. Helens,_ _which is an active volcano, is in Washington._

10. The eruption changed the mountain. The eruption happened in 1980. _____

_____

11. Huge forests were destroyed. The forests grew near the mountain. _____

_____

12. Strong winds knocked down the trees. The winds carried rocks and stone. _____

_____

13. An earthquake caused an avalanche. The earthquake started under the mountain. _____

_____

14. The avalanche rushed into the valley. The avalanche was 150 feet thick. _____

_____

Skills Review, continued

C. **Think about "The Mother Who Lost Her Daughter." Complete the sentences. Use relative clauses with *who*, *which*, or *that*.**

15. Demeter was a goddess _____who grew food for the people_____ .

16. Persephone, _____ , loved to dance.

17. One day Persephone saw a beautiful flower _____ .

18. Hades, _____ , took Persephone away.

19. The chariot _____ was made of gold.

20. Zeus felt sorry for the mortals _____ .

21. Persephone ate a pomegranate seed, _____ ,
   so she had to stay in the underworld for part of the year.

D. **Write an adverb to complete each sentence.**

22. Mount St. Helens erupted in 1980 and _____again_____ in 2004.

23. On September 23, 2004, several small earthquakes _____ shook the mountain.

24. The earthquakes happened more _____ over the next few days.

25. Scientists knew that the eruption was building _____ .

26. On October 5, 2004, Mount St. Helens erupted and sent steam, smoke, and ash

   _____ into the sky.

27. Ash fell _____ onto cars and streets even 60 miles away.

28. For six months, new lava poured out _____ .

29. _____ scientists are watching the volcano for signs of more activity.

E. **Read each sentence. Circle the correct relative pronoun.**

30. In Greek mythology, Echo was a wood nymph _____(who)/ that_____ talked a lot.

31. She lived in the woods _____who / that_____ grew on Mount Helicon.

32. One time Hera was looking for Zeus, _____who / that_____ was her husband.

33. Echo began a conversation _____who / that_____ distracted Hera.

34. Hera, _____who / that_____ was queen of the gods, punished Echo.

35. From then on Echo could only repeat things _____who / that_____ others said.

Present Perfect Tense Verbs

The **present perfect tense** tells about things that happened in the past.

- Use the present perfect tense to tell about past actions when the exact time is not known.

  Example: My teacher **has talked** about the United States in history class.

  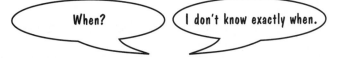

- Use the present perfect tense to tell about past actions that are still going on.

  Example: I **have lived** in the United States for my whole life.

The present perfect tense is made up of the helping verb **has** or **have** followed by the **past participle** of the verb.

- Use **has** with **he, she, it,** and singular nouns with the **past participle**.

  Example: My teacher **has helped** me learn about the United States.

  has ✚ helped ═ present perfect

- Use **have** with **I, you, we, they,** and plural nouns with the **past participle**.

  Example: I **have read** many books about American history.

  have ✚ read ═ present perfect

A. Write *has* or *have* to correctly complete each sentence.

1. My grandparents _____*have*_____ lived in the United States for a long time.

2. They _____ learned to speak English.

3. Grandma _____ visited her old country a few times.

4. She _____ told her family there all about the United States.

5. Many changes _____ happened for Grandma and Grandpa in the United States.

6. Many things _____ stayed the same, too.

Present Perfect Tense Verbs, continued

B. Complete each sentence with the present perfect tense of the verb in parentheses.

7. My class _____*has studied*_____ World War II in school. (**study**)

8. My teacher _____ us to a museum exhibit, too. (**take**)

9. Now we _____ some real uniforms from the war. (**see**)

10. I _____ a lot about World War II. (**learn**)

11. My grandma _____ some information with me. (**share**)

12. My friend and I _____ the information in our report. (**use**)

13. We _____ about the effect of World War II on America. (**talk**)

C. Rewrite each sentence using the present perfect tense.

14. I wave my flag. _*I have waved my flag.*_ _____

_____

15. She is living in the brown house. _____

_____

16. The children play in the playground. _____

_____

17. Henry studied in school. _____

_____

18. Grandpa owns a store. _____

_____

19. America helped us all! _____

_____

D. 20.–22. Answer the question in the poem. Tell a partner what America means to you. Use the present perfect tense to tell what you have done in America.

Examples: "America means that I have been free. I have learned at school.

My parents have started a business."

© Hampton-Brown

Helping Verbs (Modals)

- Some verbs are made up of two **helping verbs** and one main verb. The first helping verb is often followed by *have*.

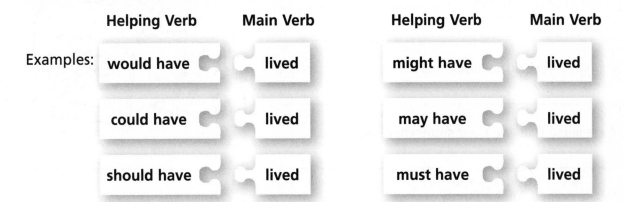

	Helping Verb	Main Verb		Helping Verb	Main Verb
Examples:	would have	lived		might have	lived
	could have	lived		may have	lived
	should have	lived		must have	lived

- Some sentences use two helping verbs with the main verb to show that one action depends upon another.

Examples:

Anne Frank **would have** **lived** in Germany, except it was not safe.

Anne's family **could have** **survived** in Amsterdam, but later it was not safe.

Action 1:	Action 2:
Germany wasn't safe. ➡	Anne's family moved.
Amsterdam wasn't safe. ➡	Anne's family didn't survive.

A. Complete the sentences. Use helping verbs with *have*.

1. I _____would have_____ felt scared if I were Anne Frank.

2. My parents _____ hidden us if they were Anne's parents.

3. My sister likes to write, so she _____ kept a diary.

4. Anne's family _____ been brave!

5. My family _____ been brave, too.

6. Maybe they _____ helped a family like Anne's.

7. Anne's family _____ lived in safety.

Helping Verbs (Modals), continued

B. Rewrite each sentence. Add two helping verbs before the main verb.

8. I bought a book about Anne Frank. _I could have_
   bought a book about Anne Frank.

9. I learned about her life. _____
   _____

10. She had a very difficult life. _____
    _____

11. She wished that she lived somewhere else. _____
    _____

12. People helped Anne's family. _____
    _____

13. Anne's family thanked them. _____
    _____

14. Anne thought about freedom. _____
    _____

15. She dreamed of better times. _____
    _____

C. 16.–20. Edit the journal entry. Use helping verbs correctly.

Journal Entry

March 10

My visit to Amsterdam is great. Today I went to see Anne Frank's house. It is a

museum now. I saw where she hid. Anne must been scared when she lived here. I

know that I have been scared if I were Anne Frank. I could gone to other museums,

but I chose this one. That's because I read her diary. It have been awful to live in

hiding. It have been nice to be free.

Revising and Editing Marks

∧	Add.
⤾	Move to here.
⌄	Replace with this.
ℐ	Take out.
⌄,	Add a comma.
⊙	Add a period.
≡	Capitalize.
/	Make lower case.

© Hampton-Brown

Two-Word Verbs

- Some phrases are **two-word verbs**.

  Examples:

Verb		Small Word		Two-Word Verb
broke	**+**	out	**=**	broke out
worked	**+**	on	**=**	worked on
turn	**+**	off	**=**	turn off
get	**+**	out	**=**	get out
look	**+**	forward	**=**	look forward

- Adding a small word to a verb creates a new meaning for the verb.

  Examples:

Anne **turned** the lamp.	**=**	Anne moved the lamp.
Anne **turned off** the lamp.	**=**	Anne made the lamp dark.
She wanted to **get** shoes.	**=**	She wanted to have shoes.
She wanted to **get out** of the annex.	**=**	She wanted to leave the annex.
She **looked** at her writing.	**=**	She saw the sentences.
She **looked forward** to writing.	**=**	She wanted to write.

A. Complete each sentence with the best two-word verb from the box. Use Handbook pages 452–453 to help you.

looked forward	got along	go out	looked over
brought up	go on	give up	got through

1. The Franks _____ brought up _____ their children in the annex.

2. Even though it was sometimes hard, they _____ with each other.

3. They _____ each day the best they could.

4. They tried not to _____ hope.

5. Anne did not _____ to school.

6. She did _____ with her writing, though.

7. Anne _____ to people reading her diary.

8. She _____ her homework carefully.

Two-Word Verbs, continued

B. Imagine you are in hiding, like Anne Frank. Use the two-word verbs in sentences about your experience. Use Handbook pages 452–453 to help you.

9. get over ___I get over being bored by reading.___
_____

10. pick on _____
_____

11. get out _____
_____

12. get through _____
_____

13. turn off _____

14. check in _____
_____

15. go out _____
_____

16. look forward _____
_____

C. 17.–22. Edit the journal entry. Use helping verbs correctly.

Journal Entry

Dear Diary,

I am sick! I have had to stay in my room all week. I feel as if I am in hiding! I cannot

wait to go on again. I have been looking forward my homework, but I'm all done now. I

am so bored that I am even looking over to going back to school! I have been picking

my brother and sister. Usually I get through with them. I am glad that I do not have

to stay inside forever! I should be able to get over tomorrow.

Revising and Editing Marks

∧   Add.
◯⤴   Move to here.
⋏   Replace with this.
⌿   Take out.
⌄   Add a comma.
⊙   Add a period.
≡   Capitalize.
/   Make lower case.

© Hampton-Brown

Present Perfect Tense Verbs

Some verbs are made up of a main verb and one or more helping verbs. The **helping verb** agrees with the **subject**.

- Use **has** with **he, she, it**, and singular nouns. Use **have** with **I, you, we, they**, and plural nouns.

  Examples: **Ted** ⸦⸧ **has lived** in Amsterdam for a long time.

  subject   helping
                    verb

  We ⸦⸧ **have visited** him there.

  subject   helping
                    verb

Use the **present perfect tense** to tell about past actions that may be continuing or whose exact time is not known.

- Use the helping verb **has** or **have** with the **past participle** of the verb to form the present perfect tense.

  Examples: He **has** ⸦⸧ **worked** at the Anne Frank museum for a long time.

  I **have** ⸦⸧ **learned** a lot about Anne Frank.

A. Write *has* or *have* to correctly complete each main verb. Then circle the subject.

1. (Anne) ___has___ heard that the Germans are losing the war.

2. She _____ started to feel hopeful.

3. Some people _____ discovered the Franks' hiding place, though.

4. They _____ told the Nazis.

5. The Nazis _____ raided the secret annex.

6. Everyone _____ become a prisoner.

7. The Franks _____ gone to concentration camps.

8. The conditions there _____ been terrible.

Present Perfect Tense Verbs, continued

B. Rewrite each sentence in the present perfect tense.

9. The Franks ended up in Auschwitz. _The Franks_
   have ended up in Auschwitz.

10. Anne worked hard with little food or water. _____

    _____

11. Many people died of hunger or sickness. _____

    _____

12. The Nazis killed many others. _____

    _____

13. The girls ended up at Bergen-Belsen. _____

    _____

14. The parents stayed at Auschwitz. _____

    _____

15. Mrs. Frank and her daughters died. _____

    _____

16. Mr. Frank survived. _____

    _____

C. 17.–26. Edit the journal entry. Use the present perfect tense correctly.

Journal Entry

June 5

I has finished reading about Anne Frank. It have been a sad story. At the end,

everyone have died except Mr. Frank. Miep Gies has saved Anne's diary, though.

Mr. Frank have decided to publish it. So the diary been published. Many people has

read it. They been amazed by Anne's courage. Her story been made into a play. Her

home become a museum. Anne has lived on through her diary. She been an inspiration

to many people.

Revising and Editing Marks	
∧	Add.
↶	Move to here.
↗	Replace with this.
ஒ	Take out.
∧,	Add a comma.
⊙	Add a period.
≡	Capitalize.
/	Make lower case.

© Hampton-Brown

Present Perfect Tense Verbs

The **present perfect tense** tells about past actions that may be continuing or whose exact time may not be known.

- Use the helping verb *has* or *have* with the **past participle** of the verb to form the present perfect tense.

  Examples: A bad thing **has happened** to Anne.

  I **have read** about it in her diary.

- Most verbs form the past tense and the past participle by adding *–ed*.

  Examples:

Verb	Past	Past Participle
pack	pack ➕ ed	packed
call	call ➕ ed	called

- Some verbs have irregular forms. See Handbook pages 450–451 for some irregular verbs.

  Examples:

Irregular Verb	Past	Past Participle
keep	kept	kept
write	wrote	written

A. Write the past participle of the verb to complete each sentence.

1. I have _____enjoyed_____ reading Anne Frank's diary.
              enjoy

2. It has _____ very sad, though.
            be

3. In some ways, Anne has _____ my hero.
                          become

4. Her diary has _____ me think about a lot of things.
                  make

5. I have _____ about the Nazis.
            think

6. I have _____ why they hurt so many people.
            wonder

7. Now that I have _____ Anne's diary, I would like to keep my own.
                    read

8. I have _____ a notebook so I can start!
            buy

Present Perfect Tense Verbs, continued

B. Rewrite each sentence in the present perfect tense. Use the past participle of the underlined verb.

9. The doorbell <u>rings</u>. The doorbell has rung. _____

10. Margot <u>appears</u> in the kitchen. _____

_____

11. Mother <u>goes</u> to see Mr. van Daan. _____

_____

12. Anne and Margot <u>wait</u> for her to return. _____

_____

13. They <u>have</u> to tiptoe downstairs. _____

_____

14. Finally Father <u>comes</u> home. _____

_____

15. Anne and her family <u>pack</u> their bags. _____

_____

16. They <u>go</u> into hiding. _____

_____

C. 17.–25. Edit the journal entry. Use the present perfect tense correctly.

Journal Entry

Dear Diary,

I has met a girl from Amsterdam. We have became good friends. She has live in my

neighborhood for about two months. Her name is Anne, just like Anne Frank. Anne

have tell me a little about Anne Frank. She been to the museum. She have see where

Anne Frank hid. Both Anne and I has read Anne Frank's diary. We have did other

fun things together, too. I am so glad that I has make a new friend!

Revising and Editing Marks

∧	Add.
↶	Move to here.
⌄	Replace with this.
⌿	Take out.
⌄	Add a comma.
⊙	Add a period.
≡	Capitalize.
/	Make lower case.

Skills Review

A. Write *has* or *have* to complete each sentence.

1. I _____have_____ studied history in school.

2. My teacher _____ taught my class about Adolf Hitler.

3. We _____ learned that he treated many people badly.

4. My grandpa _____ told me about Hitler, too.

5. He _____ visited one of the concentration camps.

6. Grandpa and Grandma _____ gone to Amsterdam.

7. They _____ seen the secret annex where Anne Frank hid.

8. The annex _____ become part of a museum.

B. Write the past participle of the verb to complete each sentence. Use Handbook pages 450–451 as necessary.

9. I have ____started____ to keep a diary.
        start

10. I have _____ something in it every night.
        write

11. My diary has _____ fun for me to have.
        be

12. No one else has _____ it, though.
        see

13. I have not _____ anyone read it.
        let

14. I have _____ my best friend about my diary.
        tell

15. She has _____ to have a diary for a long time.
        want

16. We have _____ her a diary to keep, too!
        make

17. My friend has _____ to write in her diary every night.
        begin

18. She has _____ some of her diary to her mother.
        read

19. Her mother has _____ the diary was a good idea.
        feel

Skills Review, continued

C. Rewrite each sentence in the present perfect tense.

20. Peter goes to Europe. _Peter has gone to Europe._ _____

_____

21. He visits Germany. _____

_____

22. He sees many cities there. _____

_____

23. Peter travels to Amsterdam, too. _____

_____

24. Many people tell Peter about Anne Frank's house. _____

_____

D. Complete each sentence with a helping verb from the box and *have*.

could	would	may	might	must

25. It _____ must have _____ been scary to be Jewish in Amsterdam in the 1940s.

26. I _____ tried to help families like Anne Frank's.

27. Maybe I _____ hidden them.

28. I _____ helped them escape from Amsterdam.

29. Then the families _____ survived.

E. Complete each two-word verb so that it makes sense in the sentence.

30. Marta picked _____ up _____ an old diary that she found in the attic.
       up / on

31. She checked _____ the diary.
       in / out

32. It was so interesting that Marta got _____ the diary in one day.
       out / through

33. She could not get _____ how old the diary was.
       over / ahead

34. She looked _____ to showing the diary to her mother.
       up / forward

Skills Review and Practice Tests

A. Write the relative pronoun that correctly completes the relative clause in each sentence.

1. Change can happen in cycles, _____which_____ are events that repeat.
   who / which

2. The moon, _____ we see in the night sky, changes in cycles.
   which / whose

3. My uncle, _____ is a scientist, studies the cycles of the moon.
   that / who

4. The life cycles _____ some animals go through repeat, too.
   that / who

5. The butterflies _____ fly in Mom's garden start as eggs.
   whose / that

6. An egg hatches into a larva, _____ is also called a caterpillar.
   which / who

7. The caterpillar forms a hard outer shell _____ is called a chrysalis.
   whose / that

8. This butterfly, _____ is yellow, hatched from a chrysalis.
   who / which

9. Soon it will lay eggs _____ will hatch into caterpillars.
   that / whose

10. Mom, _____ garden is a home to butterflies, explained the life cycle to me!
    who / whose

B. Use the relative clauses and the relative pronouns given to combine the sentences.

11. Some changes happen suddenly. Some changes do not happen in cycles. (**that**) _Some changes_
    that do not happen in cycles happen suddenly.

12. My grandma told me about a hurricane. My grandma lives on the coast. (**who**) _____
    _____

13. The storm changed the coastline. The storm caused big waves. (**which**) _____
    _____

14. My aunt saw changes when the volcano erupted. My aunt's home is near a volcano. (**whose**)
    _____

15. Trees were destroyed. Trees were on the mountain. (**that**) _____
    _____

C. Read the passage. Read each item carefully. Choose the best answer.
  Mark your answer.

People whose lived in ancient Greece
           1
believed that Demeter caused the seasons to
change. When Persephone disappeared,
Demeter stopped telling crops to grow. When
Persephone came back, Demeter was happy
and told crops to grow. Every year when
Persephone left, spring changed to winter.

Demeter does not cause the seasons to
change. Earth, who is our planet, orbits the
             2
sun. That causes the seasons to change!

Where I live, spring begins in March. More
sunlight, which causes warmer weather,
         3
reaches Earth. The days get longer. In June,
summer begins. My part of Earth is tilted
more toward the sun. It gets hotter, and the
days are longer. Autumn, is also called fall,
                          4
begins in September. My part of Earth is
starting to tilt farther from the sun. The
days whose were long start to get shorter.
       5
The weather gets cooler. Winter begins
in December. Earth is tilted farthest
from the sun. It is cold, and it gets dark
early! Then it is March again. People
which favorite season is spring are happy!
                6

16. In number 1, whose is best written —
    Ⓐ who
    Ⓑ which
    Ⓒ whom
    Ⓓ as it is written

17. In number 2, who is best written —
    Ⓕ that
    Ⓖ whose
    Ⓗ which
    Ⓙ as it is written

18. In number 3, which is best written —
    Ⓐ who
    Ⓑ whose
    Ⓒ whom
    Ⓓ as it is written

19. In number 4, is also called fall is best written —
    Ⓕ who is also called fall
    Ⓖ which is also called fall
    Ⓗ whose is also called fall
    Ⓙ as it is written

20. In number 5, whose were long is best written —
    Ⓐ that were long
    Ⓑ who were long
    Ⓒ were long
    Ⓓ as it is written

21. In number 6, which favorite season is spring is
    best written —
    Ⓕ favorite season is spring
    Ⓖ who favorite season is spring
    Ⓗ whose favorite season is spring
    Ⓙ as it is written

138

Skills Review and Practice Tests, continued

D. Write *has* or *have* to complete each sentence.

22. History _____has_____ had an effect on all of us.

23. Historical events _____ caused many changes in our lives.

24. People _____ moved from one country to another to escape from danger.

25. Historical inventions _____ affected our lives, too.

26. The car, for example, _____ made it easier for us to travel.

27. Some changes _____ been good.

28. Electricity _____ led to many good changes.

29. Other changes _____ caused danger to some people.

30. War _____ caused danger to many people.

31. What events _____ caused changes in your life?

E. Write the present perfect tense of the verb to complete the sentence. Use Handbook pages 450–451 as necessary.

32. Historical events ____*have led*____ to many changes.
    lead

33. People in history _____ about changes, too.
    bring

34. Anne Frank _____ a hero to many people.
    become

35. Her diary _____ us all about bravery and fairness.
    teach

36. It _____ Anne into a writer we cannot forget.
    turn

37. We _____ about right and wrong from her diary.
    learn

38. The people who helped Anne _____ changes in our lives.
    cause

39. They _____ us how to stand up for our beliefs.
    show

40. I _____ out that Johannes Kleiman was one of those people!
    find

41. I _____ that he helped keep Anne's memory alive.
    read

© Hampton-Brown

Skills Review and Practice Tests, continued

**F. Read the passage. Read each item carefully. Choose the best answer.
Mark your answer.**

Imagine it is 1933. Miep Gies <u>has meet</u> Otto Frank. She <u>have begin</u> to work for him. Miep
1 2

becomes good friends with Otto and his family. That's why she has decided to help them in July of

1942. To save the Franks from the Nazis, Miep <u>has hide</u> the Franks in the secret annex. She brings
3

them food, clothing, and news of the outside world.

Now it is August of 1944. The Nazis <u>have captured</u> the Franks. Miep goes back into the secret
4

annex. She finds Anne Frank's diary and keeps it safe. When Otto Frank returns in 1945, Miep gives

him the diary. She has not read it. Otto publishes the diary in 1947.

Now it is 2006. Miep Gies still lives in Amsterdam. Miep Gies <u>has devote</u> her life to keeping the
5

memory of the Franks alive. People <u>has recognized</u> her courage and bravery. She has received
6

many awards. She has become a legacy, just like Anne Frank. People all over the world have

learned from Miep Gies. They have learned about friendship and courage.

---

42. In number 1, <u>has meet</u> is best written —
- Ⓐ have meet
- Ⓑ have met
- Ⓒ has met
- Ⓓ as it is written

43. In number 2, <u>have begin</u> is best written —
- Ⓕ has begun
- Ⓖ has begin
- Ⓗ have begun
- Ⓙ as it is written

44. In number 3, <u>has hide</u> is best written —
- Ⓐ have hidden
- Ⓑ has hidden
- Ⓒ have hide
- Ⓓ as it is written

45. In number 4, <u>have captured</u> is best written —
- Ⓕ has captured
- Ⓖ has capture
- Ⓗ have capture
- Ⓙ as it is written

46. In number 5, <u>has devote</u> is best written —
- Ⓐ have devoted
- Ⓑ have devote
- Ⓒ has devoted
- Ⓓ as it is written

47. In number 6, <u>has recognized</u> is best written —
- Ⓕ have recognize
- Ⓖ have recognized
- Ⓗ has recognize
- Ⓙ as it is written

140

Past Perfect Tense Verbs

The **past perfect tense** shows an action that was completed before some moment in the past.

Example: We **had finished** our test before we ate lunch.

- Use the helping verb *had* plus the **past participle** of the main verb to form the past perfect tense.

  Example: Our teacher | had | | collected | the tests.

  helping verb **+** past participle

- The past participle of a regular verb ends in **–ed**.

  Example: She had | stack**ed** | the tests on her desk.

- Irregular verbs have special forms for the past participle.

Main Verb	Past Participle
see	seen
go	gone
did	done

A. Read each sentence. Circle the correct form of the past perfect verb.

1. By spring my class _____ had complete / (had completed) _____ an important school project.

2. In the winter, our class _____ had discuss / had discussed _____ many ideas.

3. Each student _____ had give / had given _____ reasons for wanting to do a project.

4. By February we _____ had voted / had voting _____ to clean up the nature trails near the school.

5. Our teacher _____ had told / had tell _____ the principal about our plan.

6. He _____ had offering / had offered _____ to go with us.

7. Also he _____ had convinced / had convince _____ other classes to join us!

8. Our teacher _____ had write / had written _____ a list of jobs.

9. She _____ had given / had gave _____ a job to each class.

10. By March we _____ had clean / had cleaned _____ every trail!

Past Perfect Tense Verbs, continued

B. 11.–25. Read one student's report about the clean-up project. Then rewrite his report. Change the underlined verbs to the past perfect tense.

> ## Our Clean-Up Project
>
> By 8:00 a.m., we <u>arrive</u> at the park. We <u>bring</u> rakes, shovels, and trash bags. Our teacher <u>gives</u> each of us a bright orange vest to wear. She <u>divides</u> us into teams of four. We <u>spend</u> about two hours cleaning. Then we <u>take</u> a break. The principal <u>hands</u> each of us a bottle of water.
>
> "Be sure to put your bottles in the trash bag," he <u>says</u> to us.
>
> We <u>go</u> back to work and <u>clean</u> for another two hours. By then we <u>collect</u> about fifty bags of trash! We <u>carry</u> the bags to the school truck. The janitor <u>loads</u> them into the truck. He <u>drives</u> them to the city dump. All of us <u>cheer</u>, "Hooray for us! The Pine Street School Clean-Up Crew!"

By 8:00 a.m., we had arrived at the park.

_____

_____

_____

_____

_____

_____

_____

_____

_____

C. Suppose you were on the clean-up project. Complete the sentences about your experience. Use verbs in the past perfect tense.

26. By 7:00 a.m., I _____ had left my house _____.

27. At the park, our teacher _____.

28. Some hikers _____.

29. Other people _____.

D. 30.–32. Tell a partner about a time you or someone else made a difference to the environment. Use verbs in the past perfect tense.

Example: "We had saved rainwater and had used it for the plants."

LEVEL B TE page T295

142

UNIT 5 | Theme 1
Build Language and Vocabulary

Name _____ Date _____

Present Perfect and Past Perfect Tenses

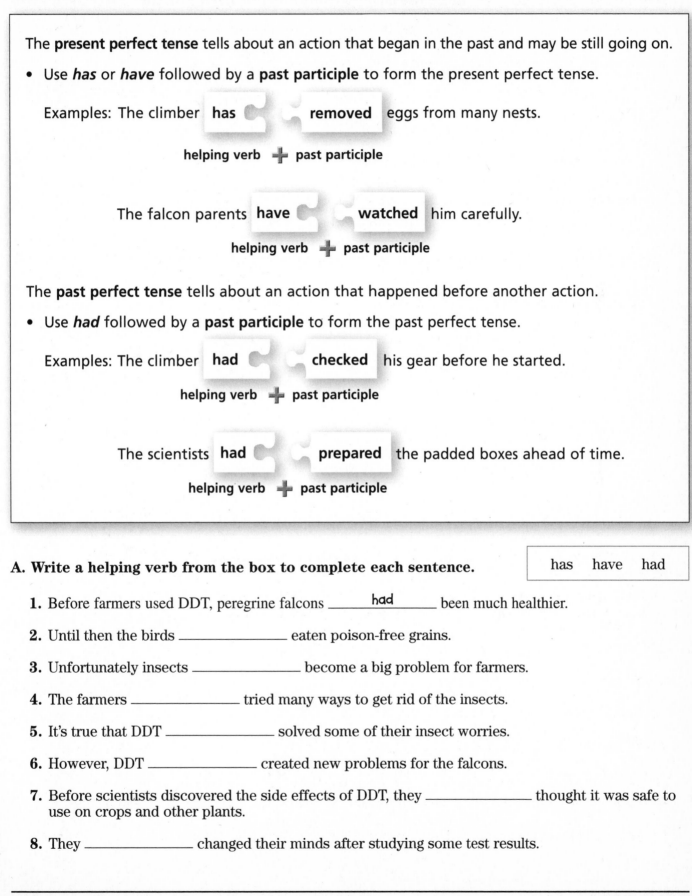

The **present perfect tense** tells about an action that began in the past and may be still going on.

- Use *has* or *have* followed by a **past participle** to form the present perfect tense.

Examples: The climber **has** **removed** eggs from many nests.

helping verb + **past participle**

The falcon parents **have** **watched** him carefully.

helping verb + **past participle**

The **past perfect tense** tells about an action that happened before another action.

- Use *had* followed by a **past participle** to form the past perfect tense.

Examples: The climber **had** **checked** his gear before he started.

helping verb + **past participle**

The scientists **had** **prepared** the padded boxes ahead of time.

helping verb + **past participle**

A. Write a helping verb from the box to complete each sentence.

| has | have | had |

1. Before farmers used DDT, peregrine falcons _____**had**_____ been much healthier.

2. Until then the birds _____ eaten poison-free grains.

3. Unfortunately insects _____ become a big problem for farmers.

4. The farmers _____ tried many ways to get rid of the insects.

5. It's true that DDT _____ solved some of their insect worries.

6. However, DDT _____ created new problems for the falcons.

7. Before scientists discovered the side effects of DDT, they _____ thought it was safe to use on crops and other plants.

8. They _____ changed their minds after studying some test results.

Present Perfect and Past Perfect Tenses, continued

B. Use the correct form of the verb and write a clause to complete the sentence. Use the tense in parentheses.

9. Before the mother falcon laid the eggs,

    <u>the parents had built the nest</u> .
         build (past perfect)

10. Then the falcon parents _____
             guard (past perfect)

_____ .

11. Until the eggs were about five days old, _____ .
                            stay (past perfect)

12. Before the falcon eggs got any older, _____ .
                          take (past perfect)

13. The climber _____ .
              put (past perfect)

14. The plaster eggs _____ .
              fool (past perfect)

15. The real eggs _____ .
              grow (past perfect)

16. Recently the baby falcons _____ .
                  go (present perfect)

17. The adult falcons _____ .
                welcome (present perfect)

18. The scientists _____ .
              help (present perfect)

C. 19.–23. Edit the journal entry below. Make sure the present perfect and past perfect tenses are used correctly.

Journal Entry

April 24

This been such an exciting day! Early this morning, I has climbed the mountain to the falcons' nest. Before I started, I had took the incubators from the lab. The climb was tough, but worth the effort. I have removed the eggs and I had replaced them with the plaster ones very quickly. As I write this, Dr. Reyes have taken good care of the eggs.

Revising and Editing Marks

∧   Add.
⤷   Move to here.
⤸   Replace with this.
♪   Take out.
⌄   Add a comma.
⊙   Add a period.
≡   Capitalize.
/   Make lower case.

Active and Passive Verbs

Verbs can be active or passive.

- A verb is **active** if the subject performs the action.

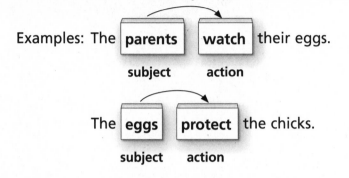

  Examples: The **parents** **watch** their eggs.
  subject action

  The **eggs** **protect** the chicks.
  subject action

- A verb is **passive** if the subject does not perform the action.

  Examples: The **eggs** **are watched** by the **parents.**
  subject action performer of the action

  The **chicks** **are protected** by the **eggs.**
  subject action performer of the action

A. Write if the verb is active or passive. If the verb is active, draw an arrow from the subject to the verb.

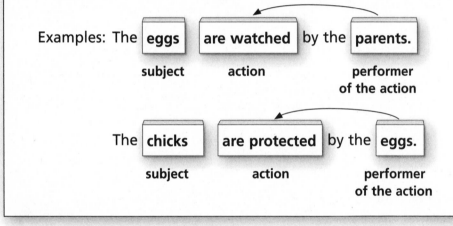

1. Golden eagles often live in the mountains. _____active_____

2. They can also be found on prairies. _____

3. Their wingspan reaches as much as seven feet across. _____

4. Small animals are eaten by these hunters. _____

5. The majestic birds are seen high in the sky. _____

6. Male and female eagles often keep the same mate for their whole lives. _____

7. Their nests are usually made on the sides of cliffs. _____

8. Quite often the couple uses the same nest for many years. _____

Active and Passive Verbs, continued

B. Rewrite each sentence. Change each sentence from the passive voice to the active voice.

9. Eggs are laid by the females only one time per year.

   The females only lay eggs one time per year.
   _____

10. The incubation of the eggs is done by the females.

   _____

   _____

11. Food is brought to the mother and chicks by the father. _____

   _____

12. Migration is sometimes done in the winter. _____

   _____

13. The effects of DDT are avoided by the eagles. _____

   _____

14. However, the eagles are sometimes shot by people. _____

   _____

15. Their beautiful feathers are sold illegally by some people. _____

   _____

16. Now eagles are protected by laws. _____

C. 17.–21. Edit the letter. Change the active voice to the passive voice.

	Revising and Editing Marks
∧	Add.
◯⤳	Move to here.
∧⛒	Replace with this.
ϟ	Take out.
∧̦	Add a comma.
⊙	Add a period.
≡	Capitalize.
/	Make lower case.

Hi Arun,

   Yesterday I saw a golden eagle!

My brother took a picture of it!

The eagle landed on a high branch.

My little sister gave a loud cry.

The eagle looked right at us!

Your friend, Keyan

© Hampton-Brown

Active and Passive Verbs

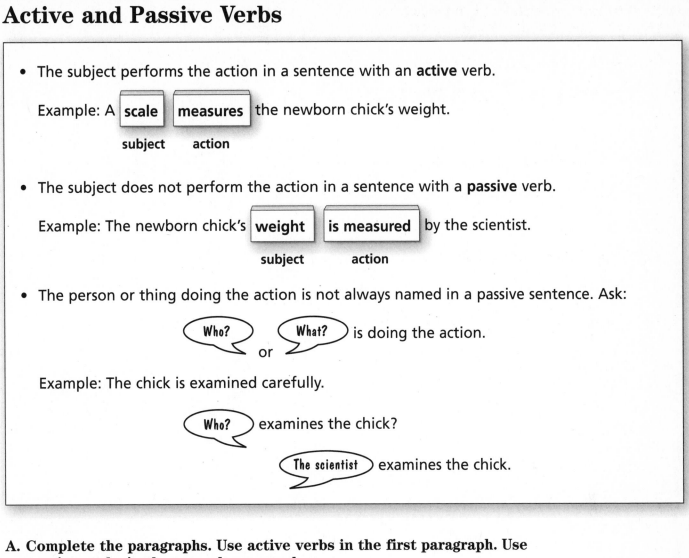

- The subject performs the action in a sentence with an **active** verb.

  Example: A ⎍scale⎍ ⎍measures⎍ the newborn chick's weight.
            subject   **action**

- The subject does not perform the action in a sentence with a **passive** verb.

  Example: The newborn chick's ⎍weight⎍ ⎍is measured⎍ by the scientist.
                       subject   **action**

- The person or thing doing the action is not always named in a passive sentence. Ask:

  Who? or What? is doing the action.

  Example: The chick is examined carefully.

  Who? examines the chick?

  The scientist examines the chick.

A. Complete the paragraphs. Use active verbs in the first paragraph. Use passive verbs in the second paragraph.

    Before the chick hatches, the chick's navel _____closes_____ . After the
                                  1.

chick hatches, its feathers _____ . Cold can harm a chick, so the chick
                         2.

_____ . When it is hungry, the chick _____ .
       3.   **4.**

Wild baby falcons _____ .
                 5.

    In the lab, _____ . The tweezers used to feed them
                6.

_____ . Falcon puppets _____ . Some
      7.   **8.**

falcon chicks without parents _____ . Wild nests
                            9.

_____ .
      10.

Active and Passive Verbs, continued

B. Read each sentence. Read the question about the sentence. Rewrite the sentence and add the answer to the question.

11. The chicks are kept warm in the wild. Who or what keeps the chicks warm in the wild?

    The mother keeps the chicks warm in the wild.

12. The chicks are cared for in the lab. Who cares for them in the lab?

    _____

13. The chicks are fed by a person using a puppet. Who feeds the chicks?

    _____

14. The chicks are fooled by the puppet. What fools the chicks?

    _____

    _____

15. Some chicks are given to the prairie falcon.
    Who gives some chicks to the prairie falcon?

    _____

    _____

16. The chicks are treated carefully. Who treats the chicks carefully?

    _____

    _____

C. 17.–21. Edit the scientist's log entry below. Change the underlined passive verbs to active verbs.

Revising and Editing Marks	
∧	Add.
⤳	Move to here.
⌃	Replace with this.
೪	Take out.
⌄	Add a comma.
⊙	Add a period.
≡	Capitalize.
/	Make lower case.

June 1

    The peregrine chicks are two weeks old now. This afternoon they were put into a prairie falcon's nest. The nest is in the wildlife preserve near the laboratory. The chicks were welcomed by the mother prairie falcon. She gave the peregrine chicks a lot of attention. Food was shared by the prairie falcon chicks. This process was taped very carefully. We need to have an accurate record of what happens to the chicks. The video was shown to our group at the lab. We are so pleased with the results of our work.

Past Perfect Tense Verbs

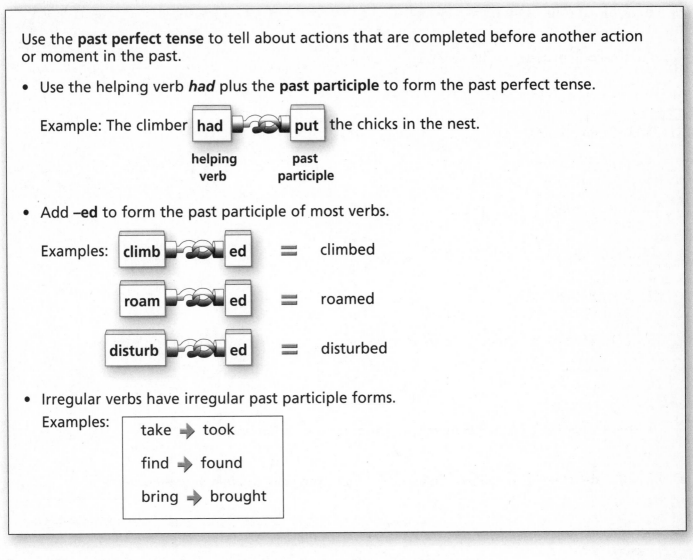

Use the **past perfect tense** to tell about actions that are completed before another action or moment in the past.

- Use the helping verb *had* plus the **past participle** to form the past perfect tense.

  Example: The climber | had |~~~~| put | the chicks in the nest.

  helping   past
  verb   participle

- Add **–ed** to form the past participle of most verbs.

  Examples: | climb |~~~~| ed | = climbed

  | roam |~~~~| ed | = roamed

  | disturb |~~~~| ed | = disturbed

- Irregular verbs have irregular past participle forms.
  Examples:

  take ➤ took

  find ➤ found

  bring ➤ brought

A. Read each irregular verb. Draw a line to the past participle.

Irregular Verbs	Past Participles
1. hold	let
2. keep	known
3. know	sent
4. feed	fed
5. let	held
6. go	left
7. leave	gone
8. send	kept

149

Past Perfect Tense Verbs, continued

B. Write the past perfect tense of the verb to complete the sentence.

9. Before the 1970s, the peregrine falcon _____had been_____ almost extinct.

be

10. Researchers in California _____ only two

find
    pairs of the birds.

11. The peregrine falcons _____ totally

disappear
    from the East Coast.

12. The government _____ peregrine falcons on the Endangered Species List.

place

13. By the mid 1970s, caring people _____ efforts to save the falcons.

begin

14. Several rescue groups _____ around the country.

form

15. In addition to breeding chicks, some rescuers _____ sick or hurt falcons.

heal

16. By 1999, these efforts _____ .

succeed

17. The peregrine falcon population _____ to 3200 birds!

grow

C. 18.–23. Edit the letter below. Make sure to use the past perfect tense correctly.

October 22

Dear Mom and Dad,

Last week Grandma and Grandpa took me to the wildlife preserve. What an interesting place! Until then I never hear about a peregrine falcon. Before we had leave the preserve, we had saw one in a bird show! Before the show, the bird trainer had tell us to watch carefully and we did. By the time we looked up, the falcon flew over our heads. I wanted to feed it, but the trainer had saying not to do that. I will tell you more when I get home next week.

Love,

Josefina

Revising and Editing Marks

∧	Add.
↶	Move to here.
∧	Replace with this.
ꝯ	Take out.
⌃	Add a comma.
⊙	Add a period.
≡	Capitalize.
/	Make lower case.

Present and Past Perfect Tense Verbs

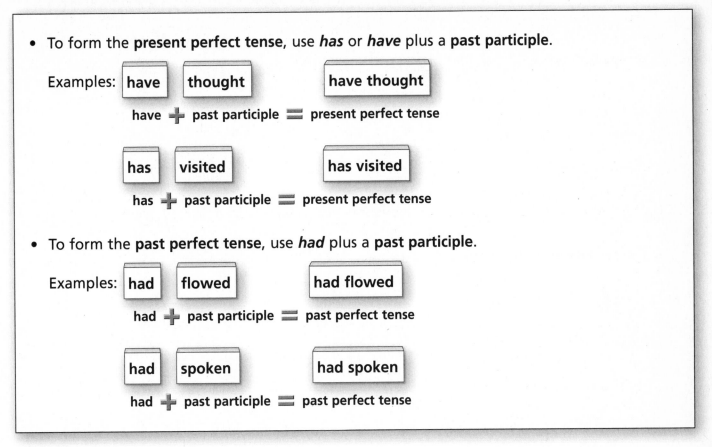

- To form the **present perfect tense**, use *has* or *have* plus a **past participle**.

  Examples: | have | | thought | | have thought |

  have + past participle = present perfect tense

  | has | | visited | | has visited |

  has + past participle = present perfect tense

- To form the **past perfect tense**, use *had* plus a **past participle**.

  Examples: | had | | flowed | | had flowed |

  had + past participle = past perfect tense

  | had | | spoken | | had spoken |

  had + past participle = past perfect tense

A. Choose the verb in the present perfect tense or past perfect tense that best completes the sentence.

1. I _____had heard_____ about Marjory Stoneman Douglas before I read her book.
   have heard / had heard

2. She _____ as a newspaper reporter in Miami, Florida, for many years.
   had worked / has worked

3. Douglas _____ the importance of the Everglades before many others did.
   have realized / had realized

4. Now many people _____ her book about the Everglades.
   have read / had read

5. By 1970, she _____ a group called "Friends of the Everglades."
   had formed / have formed

6. Since then the group's members _____ to save the Everglades.
   have worked / had worked

7. My family _____ this group recently.
   has joined / had joined

B. Rewrite each sentence twice. First rewrite it with a verb in the present perfect tense. Next rewrite it with a verb in the past perfect tense.

8. The government was building canals and dams in the Everglades. _The government has built canals and dams in the Everglades. In the 1950s, the government had built canals and dams in the Everglades._

9. The Everglades was marshy wetland. _____

10. Mrs. Douglas wrote many books. _____

11. She saw the natural beauty of the Everglades. _____

12. Mrs. Douglas convinced others to help her. _____

13. Now others praise her work. _____

C. 14.–18. Suppose you could ask these questions to Marjory Stoneman Douglas. Edit the questions. Make sure the present perfect tense and past perfect tense are used correctly.

Questions for Marjory Stoneman Douglas

What have happened recently in the Everglades?

How has you made a difference in the quality of the Everglades?

What has others done to help you?

What have been your goal when you talked to that group?

How had the Everglades improved in the last twenty years?

Revising and Editing Marks

∧	Add.
↻	Move to here.
⌄	Replace with this.
℈	Take out.
∧	Add a comma.
⊙	Add a period.
≡	Capitalize.
/	Make lower case.

© Hampton-Brown

Skills Review

A. Write the past perfect form for the verb in parentheses.

1. Before they knew what it really was, ancient sailors _____had fallen_____ in love with the manatee. (**fall**)

2. They _____ the manatees were mermaids. (**think**)

3. The sailors _____ manatees around their ships. (**see**)

4. Using their imaginations, these sea-going storytellers _____ fanciful stories about the sea animals. (**create**)

5. Once people _____ the truth about these mermaids, a different kind of interest in manatees began. (**learn**)

6. Scientists _____ the manatees' gentle nature. (**observe**)

7. Soon they _____ that the manatee was a member of the elephant family. (**discover**)

8. By the mid 1970s, the government _____ manatees to the list of protected animals. (**add**)

B. Choose a verb in the present perfect or past perfect tense and use it to complete the sentence.

9. Before people settled in the Everglades, snail kites _____had lived_____ there.
   have lived / had lived

10. In recent years, researchers _____ a lot about this bird.
    have learned / had learned

11. Scientists _____ the bird's hooked beak.
    has seen / had seen

12. The birds _____ their beaks to open snail shells.
    have used / had used

13. Then they _____ the snails from the shells.
    has removed / had removed

14. Some snail kites _____ crabs and turtles when they cannot find snails.
    have eaten / had eaten

15. In order to find food, the snail kites _____ over the Everglades marshes.
    have flown / had flown

16. In some marshes, large groups of water plants _____ the surface of the water.
    have covered / had covered

17. These plants _____ the snails from the view of the hungry birds.
    have hidden / had hidden

18. By 1967, the government _____ snail kites on the list of endangered birds.
    has included / had included

C. 19.–29. Read the passage. Underline all the verbs. Then write the verbs in the chart where they belong.

Mangrove trees <u>grow</u> in shallow swamps near oceans. Their roots are covered with salt water. Much of this salt is stored in the leaves of the trees. These leaves are dropped as the tree ages. The roots pass more salt back into the water. Mud and sand are kept in place by the strong roots.

Mangrove leaves provide food for many animals. They are eaten by monkeys and insects. In the water, crabs and moths use the fallen leaves. Herons and other birds build nests high up in mangrove trees. Safety is found by many in these trees.

Active Verbs	Passive Verbs
grow	

D. Write a verb from the box in correct active or passive form to complete each sentence.

make	find	form	threaten	need	dump

30. Plants and animals _____ need _____ the water of the Everglades.

31. A large water system _____ by the Kissimmee River, Lake Okeechobee, and the Everglades.

32. Drinking water _____ in the layer of limestone beneath the ground.

33. In the past, many waste materials _____ into the water system.

34. In 1947, the southern part of the Everglades _____ into a national park.

35. People's activities still _____ this valuable water system.

E. Write three sentences of your own. Tell how the people and projects you read about made a difference to the peregrine falcons and to the Everglades. Use verbs in the past perfect tense.

36. _____

_____

37. _____

_____

38. _____

_____

Future Perfect Tense Verbs

The **perfect tenses** show actions that happen at times other than the present.

- Verbs in **present perfect tense** and **past perfect tense** show actions that started or happened in the past.

  Examples: Brian has landed the plane.

  **present
  perfect tense**

  He had been on his way to visit his father when the pilot died.

  **past
  perfect tense**

- A verb in the **future perfect tense** shows an action that will be completed at a specific time in the future.

  Examples: By morning Brian **will have lost** all his supplies.   When?   by morning

  By afternoon he **will have started** to rebuild.   When?   by afternoon

- Use the helping verbs *will have* with the **past participle** of the main verb to form the future perfect tense.

  Examples: The tornado   **will have**   **ended**   by morning.

  Brian   **will have**   **survived**   the storm.

A. Complete the sentences with verbs in the future perfect tense. Use the past participles in parentheses.

1. By the end of the storm, many trees _____will have fallen_____ over. (**fallen**)

2. Brian's fire _____ out. (**gone**)

3. Soon after the storm, Brian _____ for his supplies. (**looked**)

4. After that he _____ that everything is gone. (**discovered**)

5. By tomorrow Brian _____ his courage. (**found**)

6. Brian _____ the challenge. (**faced**)

7. He _____ to rebuild. (**begun**)

Future Perfect Tense Verbs, continued

**B. Write the future perfect tense of the verbs to complete the sentences.
See Handbook pages 450–451 for a list of irregular past participles.**

8. By the end of our vacation, my family and I

_____will have lived_____ in the woods for a month.
                live

9. We _____ in our tent.
              sleep

10. We _____ campfires to cook our food.
              light

11. I _____ how to set up a tent.
              learn

12. We _____ to the top of the mountain.
              hike

13. We _____ under the stars.
              camp

14. My family and I _____ many challenges.
                    face

15. I hope that we _____ them all!
                   meet

C. Rewrite each sentence in the future perfect tense.

16. I finish the book Hatchet. _I will have finished the book Hatchet._

_____

17. I find out about Brian. _____

_____

18. Brian uses his hatchet. _____

_____

19. It helps him in the wilderness. _____

_____

20. Brian survives his adventure. _____

_____

**D. 21.–23. Tell a partner what you think Brian will have done by the end
of the day after the storm. Use the future perfect tense at least three times.**

Example: "Brian will have found food to eat."

Linking Verbs

- Use the **past perfect tense** to tell about a past action that was completed before another past action. Use the helping verb *had* and the **past participle** to form the past perfect tense.

  Examples: Before strawberry season, we **had** **moved** to Fresno.

  When? before strawberry season

  By sunset we **had** **arrived** at the labor camp.

  When? by sunset

- Use the **future perfect tense** to tell about an action that will be completed by a specific time in the future. Use *will have* and the **past participle** to form the future perfect tense.

  Examples: Before noon the temperature **will have** **risen** to 100 degrees.

  When? before it gets to be noon

  By the time he eats dinner, Panchito **will have** **worked** hard all day.

  When? before he eats dinner

A. Write *had* or *will have* to complete the sentences correctly.

1. My mother made pies with strawberries that we _____had_____ picked.

2. Before we picked them, the strawberries _____ gotten ripe.

3. By tonight we _____ eaten another pie.

4. By next week, the strawberries _____ stopped growing.

5. It is lucky that my mother _____ frozen some pies.

6. Soon we _____ eaten the very last strawberry pie!

7. By then we _____ picked some blueberries.

8. By next month, my mother _____ made blueberry pies!

Linking Verbs, continued

B. Write the past perfect tense or the future perfect tense of the verbs to complete the sentences correctly. See Handbook pages 450–451 for a list of irregular past participles.

9. For a while, Panchito _____had picked_____ strawberries. (**pick**)

10. Soon he _____ to a new place. (**move**)

11. By tomorrow morning, he _____ to pick a new crop. (**start**)

12. By noon the temperature _____ to almost 100 degrees. (**rise**)

13. By dark the grapes _____ red. (**turn**)

14. By tomorrow night, Panchito _____ a lot of grapes. (**pick**)

15. Before he goes to sleep, he _____ a special dinner. (**eat**)

16. For dinner Mamá _____ rice and tortillas with "chile con carne." (**cook**)

17. In the past, Panchito _____ hard in the strawberry fields. (**work**)

18. By the end of grape season, he _____ a lot of time picking grapes. (**spend**)

19. Often Panchito thought about the fields that _____ full of strawberries and grapes. (**be**)

C. 20.–27. Edit the journal entry. Use the past perfect and future perfect tenses correctly.

Journal Entry

I am working hard picking grapes today. I went out to the vineyard before the sun will have risen. Before I stopped for lunch, the temperature risen a lot. Before I go home this afternoon, it have risen even more! When I stopped to write this journal entry, I already had pick hundreds of grapes. Before I eat dinner, I picked hundreds more. Before I go to bed, I will have eat my dinner. My mom have make tortillas. I wish I eaten a bigger breakfast this morning. Maybe then I would not be so hungry right now!

Revising and Editing Marks

∧	Add.
⟳	Move to here.
⌄	Replace with this.
℘	Take out.
∧	Add a comma.
⊙	Add a period.
≡	Capitalize.
/	Make lower case.

© Hampton-Brown

Future Perfect Tense Verbs

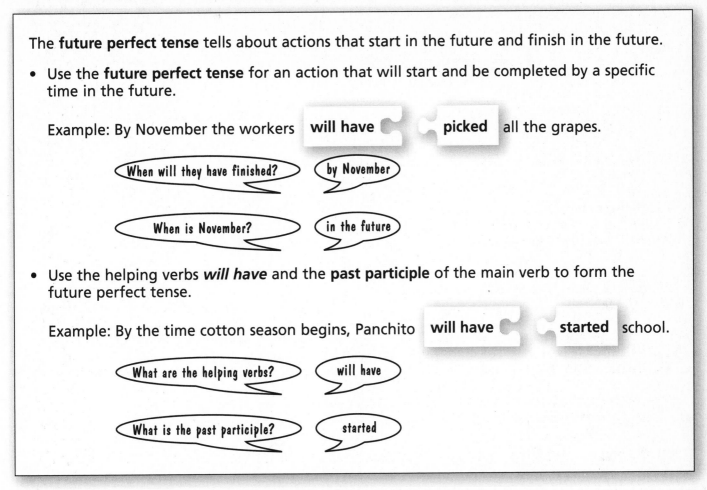

The **future perfect tense** tells about actions that start in the future and finish in the future.

- Use the **future perfect tense** for an action that will start and be completed by a specific time in the future.

  Example: By November the workers **will have** **picked** all the grapes.

  When will they have finished?   by November

  When is November?   in the future

- Use the helping verbs **will have** and the **past participle** of the main verb to form the future perfect tense.

  Example: By the time cotton season begins, Panchito **will have** **started** school.

  What are the helping verbs?   will have

  What is the past participle?   started

A. Write the future perfect tense of the verbs to complete the sentences correctly. See Handbook pages 450–451 for a list of irregular past participles.

1. By the end of the day, Mom and I _____will have picked_____ grapes. (**pick**)

2. Before we pick, we _____ to the vineyard. (**drive**)

3. Before we stop picking, we _____ many grapes! (**eat**)

4. By the time I go to bed, we _____ all the grapes. (**wash**)

5. By tomorrow night, I _____ Mom. (**help**)

6. We _____ a lot of grape jam. (**make**)

7. By the end of the week, we _____ some of our jam to our friends. (**give**)

8. We _____ some for ourselves, too. Yum! (**keep**)

Future Perfect Tense Verbs, continued

B. Use the future perfect tense to complete the sentences about Panchito and "The Circuit."

9. Before he gets on the bus, Panchito _____

_____ will have eaten breakfast _____ .

10. Before lunch Panchito _____

_____ .

11. By the time recess is over, Panchito _____

_____ .

12. By the end of the month, Mr. Lema _____

_____ .

13. Before long Panchito _____

_____ .

14. Before Panchito becomes a professor, he _____

_____ .

15. By the time I finish reading "The Circuit," I _____

_____ .

C. 16.–22. Edit the letter. Use the future perfect tense correctly.

Dear Grandma,

    I love strawberries! By the end of strawberry season, I will have pick a lot of them. I will eaten a lot of them, too! A bit after strawberry season ends, blueberry season will have begin. I love blueberries! By the end of blueberry season, I have made blueberry pies! By the end of September, apple season will started. I love apples! By the end of apple season, I will have bring home a lot of apples. I will have cook a lot of applesauce.

Love,

Ana

Revising and Editing Marks

∧	Add.
↰	Move to here.
⌃	Replace with this.
ॄ	Take out.
⌄	Add a comma.
⊙	Add a period.
≡	Capitalize.
/	Make lower case.

Skills Review

A. Read each sentence. Circle the correct future perfect tense verb.

1. By tonight I _____ (will have left) / will have leave _____ for China.

2. I _____ will be pack / will have packed _____ my bags.

3. I _____ will have gone / will have go _____ to the airport.

4. The plane _____ will have take / will have taken _____ off.

5. By next week, I _____ will have visited / will have visiting _____ some cities.

6. I _____ will traveled / will have traveled _____ to the countryside, too.

7. I hope that I _____ will be hear / will have heard _____ some Chinese folk tales.

8. By next month, I _____ will have return / will have returned _____ home.

9. My parents _____ will have missed / will have miss _____ me.

10. I _____ will have had / will had have _____ a good time.

**B. Write the past perfect tense of the verb to complete each sentence.
Use Handbook pages 450–451 as necessary.**

11. Before I left China, I _____ had heard _____ a folk tale.

               hear

12. A long time ago, a man _____ in China.

              live

13. His wife _____ very clever.

          be

14. One day the magistrate _____ to town.

              come

15. Before that the man _____ scrolls up to honor his wife.

            put

16. After the magistrate saw the scrolls, he _____ the man to come to his office.

                order

17. At his office, he _____ the man three impossible tasks.

          give

18. The man _____ his wife his problem.

       tell

19. Before long his wife _____ his problem.

          solve

20. She _____ of creative ways to stop the punishment.

       think

Skills Review, continued

C. Write the past perfect tense or the future perfect tense of the verbs to complete the sentences correctly.

21. By tomorrow I ___will have finished___ my report on folk tales. (**finish**)

22. I _____ my own folk tale before tomorrow, too. (**write**)

23. Before I started, I _____ only a few folk tales. (**hear**)

24. I _____ about "The Clever Wife" before I started my report. (**know**)

25. By the time I finish, I _____ a lot of folk tales. (**read**)

26. Before I started, Mom _____ me I would like folk tales. She was right! (**tell**)

D. Rewrite each sentence in the future perfect tense and in the past perfect tense.

Fu-hsing runs to his wife with questions.

27. ___Fu—hsing will have run to his wife with questions.___

28. _____

She thinks of a solution.

29. _____

30. _____

Fu-hsing is proud of his wife.

31. _____

32. _____

E. Use the future perfect tense to complete the sentences.

33. By tomorrow Fu-hsing _____ will have visited the magistrate _____.

34. Before then his wife _____.

35. By the end of the story, the magistrate _____.

36. Before the story ends, I _____.

© Hampton-Brown

Skills Review and Practice Tests

A. Write the verb that correctly completes each sentence. Then circle all the verbs that are in the past perfect tense.

1. Pollution _____ *has affected* _____ our environment.
   has affected / have affected

2. Before people started using DDT, peregrines _____ many babies.
   have had / had had

3. Since DDT, peregrines _____ trouble hatching their eggs.
   has had / have had

4. Before the Kissimmee River was turned into a canal, it _____ clean water
   has brought / had brought
   to Lake Okeechobee.

5. Since then it _____ pollution to the lake.
   has carried / had carried

6. Living things always _____ clean air, water, and soil to live.
   had needed / have needed

7. Now some air, water, and soil _____ dirty.
   have become / had become

B. Rewrite each sentence in the present perfect tense. Then write it in the past perfect tense.

Rafael thinks about the environment.

8. _Rafael has thought about the environment._

9. _____

He and his friends make a difference.

10. _____

11. _____

They clean up the neighborhood park.

12. _____

13. _____

The mayor thanks them.

14. _____

15. _____

C. Read the passage. Read each item carefully. Choose the best answer.
Mark your answer.

Even before I read "Saving the Peregrine Falcon," I <u>has known</u> about endangered
<u>1</u>
animals. A while ago, I <u>have read</u> a book about
<u>2</u>
endangered species. Tigers, giant pandas, and rhinoceroses are all endangered. People <u>have moved</u> into their habitats. Pollution has
<u>3</u>
harmed them, too. I have tried to make a difference. Yesterday I joined a wildlife organization. Before that I <u>has adopted</u> a tiger.
<u>4</u>
Now twice a year, I get updates about my tiger. I find out whether it is still surviving in the wild. I find out what I can do to help other animals.

I <u>had try</u> to make a difference in other
<u>5</u>
ways, too. I'm trying to stop water pollution. Water pollution can hurt or kill animals that live in ponds, lakes, or the sea. It is harmful to plants, too. Last year I <u>have learned</u> about
<u>6</u>
water pollution in school. Now I'm taking steps to make a difference. I do not ever throw things into the ocean or a lake. I always turn off the faucet when I'm not using the water. I also have helped clean up our local river. I think it is important for everyone to make a difference. What can you do?

16. In number 1, <u>has known</u> is best written —
- Ⓐ had know
- Ⓑ have known
- Ⓒ had known
- Ⓓ as it is written

17. In number 2, <u>have read</u> is best written —
- Ⓕ had read
- Ⓖ has read
- Ⓗ have readed
- Ⓙ as it is written

18. In number 3, <u>have moved</u> is best written —
- Ⓐ have move
- Ⓑ has moved
- Ⓒ had move
- Ⓓ as it is written

19. In number 4, <u>has adopted</u> is best written —
- Ⓕ had adopt
- Ⓖ had adopted
- Ⓗ have adopted
- Ⓙ as it is written

20. In number 5, <u>had try</u> is best written —
- Ⓐ have tried
- Ⓑ have try
- Ⓒ has tried
- Ⓓ as it is written

21. In number 6, <u>have learned</u> is best written —
- Ⓕ have learn
- Ⓖ has learned
- Ⓗ had learned
- Ⓙ as it is written

164

Skills Review and Practice Tests, continued

D. Write the past perfect tense or the future perfect tense of the verbs to complete the sentences correctly.

22. By tomorrow Julio _____will have pushed_____ past his limits. (**push**)

23. Tomorrow night he _____ his first big race. (**complete**)

24. Before Julio watched the big race last year, he already _____ to run. (**decide**)

25. Even back then, he _____ to train. (**start**)

26. By the time Julio finishes the race, he _____ a huge goal. (**accomplish**)

27. Before last year, Julio _____ his challenge. (**face**)

28. Tomorrow he _____ his challenge. (**meet**)

29. Before this I _____ proud of Julio. (**be**)

30. Before he is done, Julio _____ great courage. (**show**)

E. Use the future perfect tense to complete the sentences about challenges.

31. By tomorrow _____ I will have run my fastest mile ever _____

    _____ .

32. By the end of the year, _____

    _____ .

33. By the time I grow up, _____

    _____ .

34. In the future, I hope that _____

    _____ .

35. When I am in college, _____

    _____ .

36. Someday maybe _____

    _____ .

F. Read the passage. Read each item carefully. Choose the best answer. Mark your answer.

People often push past their limits to meet a challenge. Athletes face physical challenges. By the time the competition comes, they <u>will practiced</u> a lot. Before they compete, they
<u>will had pushed</u> past their limits.

    Migrant workers face physical challenges, too. Before Francisco Jiménez became a writer, he <u>been</u> a migrant worker. He and his family moved from camp to camp, following the harvest. Francisco struggled to learn English. He tried hard to push past his limits. By the time he left high school, all his learning <u>have helped</u> him leave the life of a migrant worker behind. Francisco Jiménez had faced his challenges.

    What challenges do you face? Do you have a problem? You can work hard. Before you know it, you <u>will solved</u> your problem! Maybe you want to learn to do something new. Before today you <u>will try</u>. Try again! Push your limits. Maybe by tomorrow, you will have met your challenge!

37. In number 1, <u>will practiced</u> is best written —
- Ⓐ will had practiced
- Ⓑ will practice
- Ⓒ will have practiced
- Ⓓ as it is written

38. In number 2, <u>will had pushed</u> is best written —
- Ⓕ will have pushed
- Ⓖ will have push
- Ⓗ had push
- Ⓙ as it is written

39. In number 3, <u>been</u> is best written —
- Ⓐ will have been
- Ⓑ had been
- Ⓒ will be
- Ⓓ as it is written

40. In number 4, <u>have helped</u> is best written —
- Ⓕ had helped
- Ⓖ will have helped
- Ⓗ have help
- Ⓙ as it is written

41. In number 5, <u>will solved</u> is best written —
- Ⓐ will have solve
- Ⓑ had solve
- Ⓒ will have solved
- Ⓓ as it is written

42. In number 6, <u>will try</u> is best written —
- Ⓕ will have tried
- Ⓖ had tried
- Ⓗ had try
- Ⓙ as it is written